MW01063372

Those of us who continually st̲u̲
we, like many others, have not fu
and every circumstance" with th
sword of the Spirit—the Word of God—Megan Hill has given us
a wise and beautifully written daily devotional to help us attain
this important Christian virtue. Its practical insights and applications, its simplicity and depth, its conviction and comfort will
make this a daily devotional that I will return to often in my ongoing struggle for the great gain of godliness with contentment.
  —**William Barcley**, Senior Pastor, Sovereign Grace Presbyte-
    rian Church, Charlotte, North Carolina; Author, *The Secret
    of Contentment*

Our hearts are often prone to discontent. We want what others
have and think that our lives would be better if only that one thing
would change (and that one thing sometimes varies from week
to week). Megan Hill's new devotional helps readers to see the
source of discontent and paints a picture of biblical contentment
rooted in the gospel. *Contentment: Seeing God's Goodness* helps
those who are longing to shed the weight of discontent by point-
ing them to the soul-satisfying contentment found in Jesus Christ.
  —**Christina Fox**, Counselor; Author, *A Heart Set Free* and
    *Closer Than a Sister*

While discontent can spring up like weeds in a garden, contentment is a cultivated fruit, learned through study and practice.
Megan Hill's new devotional *Contentment: Seeing God's Goodness*
overflows with wisdom, truth, and practical applications. These
daily readings refocus our gaze off of ourselves (or our neighbor's
cute new coat) and onto the goodness and faithfulness of our God.
It's a needed and helpful book, and I highly recommend it.
  —**Melissa Kruger**, Author, *The Envy of Eve: Finding Content-
    ment in a Covetous World*; Women's Ministries Coordinator,
    Uptown Church, Charlotte, North Carolina

Megan Hill exposes the lie that seduces so many of us, demonstrating that a change in our circumstances will *not* improve our lives. With clear, practical, biblical reflection, Hill leads us to the greener pastures of Christian contentment. But she doesn't simply tell us to "stop our complaining"; she tells us to embrace Christ, the suffering yet contented Savior. I am glad for this resource that teaches us to live his life of holy, surrendered desire.

—**Jen Pollock Michel**, Author, *Teach Us to Want* and *Keeping Place*

"Be content." "Pursue contentment." "Repent of discontent." We've all heard the exhortations and rebukes. We all agree with them. "But *how*?" we cry. How do we get there?

Megan Hill comes to the rescue with a practical daily devotional full of how-to's and why-to's. But, more importantly, she shows that the remedy for discontent lies ultimately not within the "how" and "why" of a daily technique but in the "who" of a daily relationship with Jesus Christ.

—**David Murray**, Professor of Old Testament and Practical Theology, Puritan Reformed Theological Seminary; Author, *The Happy Christian* and *Christians Get Depressed Too*

# CONTENTMENT

31-DAY DEVOTIONALS FOR LIFE

A Series

DEEPAK REJU
Series Editor

*Addictive Habits: Changing for Good,* by David R. Dunham
*After an Affair: Pursuing Restoration,* by Michael Scott Gembola
*Contentment: Seeing God's Goodness,* by Megan Hill
*Doubt: Trusting God's Promises,* by Elyse Fitzpatrick
*Grief: Walking with Jesus,* by Bob Kellemen
*Pornography: Fighting for Purity,* by Deepak Reju

# CONTENTMENT

# SEEING GOD'S GOODNESS

## MEGAN HILL

P U B L I S H I N G
P.O. BOX 817 • PHILLIPSBURG • NEW JERSEY 08865-0817

For my parents, Brad and Patsy Evans,
who taught me by exhortation and example to
believe that God always gives what is best.

Printed in the United States of America

**Library of Congress Cataloging-in-Publication Data**

Names: Hill, Megan, 1978- author.
Title: Contentment : seeing God's goodness / Megan Hill.
Description: Phillipsburg : P&R Publishing, 2018. | Series: 31-day devotionals for life | Includes bibliographical references.
Identifiers: LCCN 2018028216| ISBN 9781629954882 (pbk.) | ISBN 9781629954899 (epub) | ISBN 9781629954905 (mobi)
Subjects: LCSH: Contentment--Religious aspects--Christianity. | Devotional exercises.
Classification: LCC BV4647.C7 H55 2018 | DDC 242--dc23
LC record available at https://lccn.loc.gov/2018028216

# Contents

**Cultivating a Thankful Heart**

**Pursuing Contentment in Specific Circumstances**

# Tips for Reading This Devotional

EARLY IN OUR MARRIAGE, my wife and I lived on the top floor of a town house, in a small one-bedroom apartment. Whenever it rained, leaks in the roof would drip through the ceiling and onto our floors. I remember placing buckets in different parts of the apartment and watching the water slowly drip, one drop at a time. I put large buckets out and thought, *It'll take a while to fill them.* The water built up over time, and often I was surprised at how quickly those buckets filled up, overflowing if I didn't pay close enough attention.

This devotional is just like rain filling up a bucket. It's slow, and it builds over time. Just a few verses every day. Drip. Drip. Drip. Just a few drops of Scripture daily to satiate your parched soul.

*We start with Scripture.* God's Word is powerful. In fact, it's the most powerful force in the entire universe.[1] It turns the hearts of kings, brings comfort to the lowly, and gives spiritual sight to the blind. It transforms lives and turns them upside down. We know that the Bible is God's very own words, so we read and study it to know God himself.

*Our study of Scripture is practical.* Theology should change how we live. It's crucial to connect the Word with your struggles. Often, as you read this devotional, you'll see the word *you* because Megan speaks directly to you, the reader. Each reading contains reflection questions and a practical suggestion. You'll get much more from this experience if you answer the questions and do the practical exercises. Don't skip them. Do them for the sake of your own soul.

*Our study of Scripture is worshipful.* Fundamentally, any struggle with contentment and ingratitude is a worship problem. We've lost our orientation toward the One who should rule our lives, and we need to turn back to him. The Word points us to Christ, who rescues us from our plight and reorients our life. The goal of your time in God's Word should always be worship. As you grow in your affections for Christ, the King, you put to death your disordered desires and ungrateful attitudes. The power of a greater affection for Christ can transform your soul. You'll grow in your contentment and gratitude as you fix your eyes on the cross. Adore Christ. Love him. Cherish him. Praise him. Honor him. Give your whole life to him. Don't hold anything back.

If you find this devotional helpful (and I trust that you will!), reread it in different seasons of your life. Work through it this coming month, and then come back to it a year from now, to remind yourself how to fight for contentment.

This devotional is *not* meant to be a comprehensive guide to contentment. Good volumes are already written for that purpose. Buy them and make good use of them. You'll see several resources listed at the end of the book.

That's enough for now. Let's begin.

Deepak Reju

# Introduction

DISCONTENT CAN STRIKE at any time. On a Monday morning, the alarm goes off, and discontent is ready to pounce. Anything can invite an attack—a careless slosh from your coffee mug, a terse text from your spouse, a towering mountain of laundry on the basement floor—and you are frustrated with your life before you even walk out the door. By the time the doctor's office calls with your test results or the mail delivery brings a new round of bills, you are wishing for a new life entirely. Even something as simple as an unexpected rain shower can unleash thunderclouds in your heart. Just a few hours ago you were joyfully worshipping God in the assembly of the saints at church, and today you are thoroughly disappointed about how this same God is ordering events.

And it doesn't stop there. Throughout our days, discontent waits for all of us. Whether we are young or old, alone or in a group, relaxing or working, we face circumstances that frustrate our expectations of what life should be like.

Once it takes hold of our hearts, discontent quickly leads to other sins. Because we fundamentally distrust what God is doing in and for us, our hearts give way to worry. Every new circumstance feels surprising and potentially harmful. Everything from the flu to the presidential election brings an onslaught of uncertainty. We do not believe that God is caring for us, and we have little confidence that the events in our lives will be for our good, so our minds and hearts spin with anxiety.

Dissatisfied with our own situation, we look around at the lives of others and add the sin of envy. We covet the lives of our friends and neighbors—people who seem to have everything we want and more. We also covet the lives of strangers—the happy couple with the gorgeous HGTV home or the alumnus whose fast-track career was lauded in the latest university publication. We lust after their accomplishments or relationships or finances, increasing our discontent with our own.

Frustrated and disappointed, we also fall into the snare of complaining. Seemingly every situation releases a sigh from our hearts. The weather is too cold. The gray hairs are too plentiful. The kids are too energetic. The pay is paltry, the hours over-long, the commute a total waste. Like the Israelites in the wilderness, we give voice to our discontent with grumbling—accusing God of mishandling our lives, and demanding that he give us what we want.

Discontent—and its evil companions—are everywhere.

But if discontent waits just around the next corner, grace does too. At every moment, in every one of life's circumstances, the Lord is ready with forgiveness (see Neh. 9:17), encouragement (see Rom. 15:5), strength (see Phil. 4:13), and love (see Rom. 8:38–39). The God who made you and sustains you is able to make grace abound to you for all things at all times (see 2 Cor. 9:8). In the fight against discontent, you are never alone.

Over the next thirty-one days, we will be studying the grace of contentment and seeking, by the help of the Holy Spirit, to rest content in God's sovereignty over the circumstances of our lives. You may want to use this devotional on your own, as a part of your daily prayer and Bible reading. But since temptation to discontent is common to all of us (see 1 Cor. 10:13), you may also want to do this study with a friend or a small group, encouraging one another to contentment in the specific areas where each person struggles.

In our quest for "a tranquil heart" (Prov. 14:30), we will meditate on what the Bible says about the dangers of discontent and the joy of contentment. Each daily reading and its application section contain Scripture; read those verses carefully. It is the Word of God that can constrain and compel us to obedience in this area. It is the Word of God that the Spirit will use to bring forth contentment in our hearts.

We will begin the month by considering the value of contentment (days 1–3). Contentment is simple, but it isn't easy. We must allow the Bible's teaching to impress on our hearts the importance and blessedness of humbly receiving all things from God's loving hand. Next we will look to Christ for our example and for help in the fight for contentment (days 4–7). Christ was the only perfectly content man, and he is our best ally as we pursue a contented heart. Then we will turn our eyes to our own circumstances and will consider how God would have us understand the events he brings into our lives (days 8–12). Of course contentment does not mean that we avoid all desire, and so we will also search the Bible to discover what desires we ought to have (days 13–18). And, having submitted our righteous desires to God, we will seek to cultivate a thankful heart—which is the antidote to grumbling (days 19–23). Finally, we will look at specific circumstances of life in which contentment seems to be difficult—areas like work, money, and relationships—and we will see how the Bible directs our hearts toward trust in God (days 24–31).

We have one clear aim. No matter what situation we find ourselves in, we want to be able to say, "I have learned in whatever situation I am to be content. I know how to be brought low, and I know how to abound. In any and every circumstance, I have learned the secret of facing plenty and hunger, abundance and need. I can do all things through him who strengthens me" (Phil. 4:11–13).

*"Christian contentment is that sweet, inward, quiet, gracious frame of spirit, which freely submits to and delights in God's wise and fatherly disposal in every condition."*

Jeremiah Burroughs

# THE VALUE OF CONTENTMENT

# DAY 1

# Abundant Life

*A tranquil heart gives life to the flesh, but envy*
*makes the bones rot. (Prov. 14:30)*

I THOUGHT THAT the coat would change everything. Red canvas, with large pockets and a brown corduroy collar, this coat was just what every student in my seventh-grade class wanted. I was absolutely sure that owning this coat would lead me into a new life. When I wore it, I would be popular, beautiful, talented. With a coat like that, people would invite me to take long autumn strolls down New England country roads or to stand, smiling and radiant, in their immaculate horse barns. When I wore it, I would be a different person entirely.

I still have the coat. It hangs in the back of a closet, and I haven't worn it in the last twenty years. Needless to say, I can't recall any significant change that happened to me because of the coat. I come across it occasionally, when I am looking for the Christmas decorations or the spare sheets, and I remember how I once thought it would finally give me the life I wanted.

Setting my hope on a piece of clothing seems silly now, but over the years I have nevertheless repeatedly convinced myself that a change in my circumstances would make everything better. I've believed that getting married or having a baby or succeeding in my job or moving or mastering a new skill would be *the* way to a fulfilling life. And, every time, I have been disappointed.

In what seems like upside-down logic, the Scriptures make it clear that a better life consists not in chasing something new but in being contented with the way things are. The way to abundant life, says Proverbs, is a tranquil heart.

If you have picked up this book, it is probably because you are interested in cultivating contentment in your heart. Perhaps you, like me, have already discovered that the perfect coat (or marriage or job or church) will not ultimately satisfy you. Perhaps you have wasted much time looking longingly over your neighbor's fence, and you sadly know the truth of today's verse: "envy makes the bones rot." Perhaps you would like to have a tranquil heart, but you don't know where to begin.

The good news for each of us is that the Lord provides everything we need for contentment. Christ came to earth, lived a life of perfect obedience, died on the cross, and was raised again so that we might be freed from envy and find satisfaction in him. Moreover, he gives us his indwelling Spirit to warn us against grumbling and to nurture contentment in our hearts as we learn from his Word. By God's grace, we can have the tranquil heart that yields abundant life. Be encouraged!

**Reflect:** What changes to your circumstances have you wrongly believed would bring you abundant life? What was the ultimate impact of those changes? Make a list of the ways you notice "rot" in your "bones" as a result of discontent.

**Reflect:** How has the Spirit helped you to fight sin and cultivate holiness in other areas of your life? How can his past faithfulness be an encouragement to you as you pursue contentment?

**Act:** Memorize this classic definition of contentment, or post it somewhere you will see it frequently: "Christian contentment is that sweet, inward, quiet, gracious frame of spirit, which freely submits to and delights in God's wise and fatherly disposal in every condition."[1]

# DAY 2

# A Weightless Heart

*Therefore, since we are surrounded by so great a cloud of witnesses, let us also lay aside every weight, and sin which clings so closely, and let us run with endurance the race that is set before us. (Heb. 12:1)*

JOHN BUNYAN'S FAMOUS allegory, *Pilgrim's Progress*, begins with its main character, Christian, suffering under the weight of a heavy burden tied to his back. It causes him distress, slows his movements, prevents him from taking joy in the ordinary blessings of his life, and puts him in danger. His burden, of course, is sin.

After trying and failing to rid himself of his burden, Christian finds relief from it at the cross of Christ. And when it rolls away, Christian is immediately refreshed. Bunyan tells us that he was "glad and lightsome," "gave three leaps for joy," and went on his way singing.[1]

The author of Hebrews likewise describes sin as a clinging weight that keeps us from joyful perseverance in the life of faith. One such burdensome sin is discontent. When we are discontent, we are in a constant state of distress, anxiety, and regret. Failing to trust God's essential goodness, we become suspicious of him and cannot enjoy him or his many blessings. We are focused on our own circumstances and do not love others well.

Thankfully, the Lord has warned us of sin's crushing weight. He has given us his Spirit to help us lay it aside (see Rom. 8:13), and he has even given us the enduring testimony of others who have experienced the power of God to free them from sin in their own lives.

One member of the cloud of witnesses is Job. At the beginning of his story, he had children, servants, and livestock in abundance (see Job 1:1–3). And yet we all know what happened—in a single day, all these good things were taken away from Job (see vv. 13–19).

Job's response encourages us: "And he said, 'Naked I came from my mother's womb, and naked shall I return. The LORD gave, and the LORD has taken away; blessed be the name of the LORD.' In all this Job did not sin or charge God with wrong" (vv. 21–22). How easy it would have been for Job to allow the sin of grumbling to weigh down his soul! But because he "feared God and turned away from evil" (v. 1), he placed the highest value on a clear conscience and a right relationship with God. Even under great affliction, Job experienced the blessing of a weightless heart.

**Reflect:** Discontent acts as a deadly weight, hampering our growth in righteousness and dragging us away from joy in Christ. How has discontent weakened your endurance in the Christian race?

**Reflect:** Read Job 1. Meditate on the fact that Job stands beside you as a witness to the Spirit's power to strip away the burden of our sin and bring contentment to our hearts.

**Act:** In *Discovering The Joy of a Clear Conscience*, Christopher Ash writes, "I get a clear conscience today the same way I got a cleansed conscience at the start: by turning from known sin and trusting afresh in the blood of Jesus Christ."[2] Deal with your discontent today the same way you did on the day you first believed. Then rejoice in the blessing of a weightless heart.

# DAY 3

# Contentment Is Great Gain

*Godliness with contentment is great gain, for we brought nothing into
the world, and we cannot take anything out of the world. But if we have
food and clothing, with these we will be content. (1 Tim. 6:6–8)*

ONCE EVERY YEAR, the fast food restaurant Chick-Fil-A
offers a free meal to anyone who comes to the restaurant dressed
as a cow. Waiting in the long line, some people appear unabash-
edly delighted to be bovine for a day, while others obviously feel
a little silly. Not everyone finds it easy to appear in public wearing
head-to-toe Holstein, yet thousands of people dress up anyway,
motivated by the promise of free chicken nuggets and waffle fries.
When there's something to be gained, we are usually willing to
make ourselves uncomfortable.

Today's passage promises us that the often-difficult discipline
of contentment will bring us "great gain" (v. 6). When we understand our own dependence on God (see v. 7) and are satisfied
with his provision for our needs (see v. 8), we gain a reward more
valuable than anything else we might lack. Truly, the one who
pursues contentment will accumulate "treasures in heaven, where
neither moth nor rust destroys and where thieves do not break in
and steal" (Matt. 6:20).

In the 1600s, the Puritan Jeremiah Burroughs made a list of
contentment's "excellencies."[1] As we consider a few of these God-
given rewards, allow them to motivate you toward contented
godliness:

1. *Contentment makes us ready to worship God.* When we worship, in private or in public, we acknowledge that God
   alone is God and that we are his humble creatures who

owe him our very selves. If we are contented, we will be eager to sing and pray and listen to the God who does all things well (see Job 1:20–21).

2. *Contentment allows us to experience and display God's grace.* Contentment does not come naturally to anyone. Apart from grace, all people grumble and complain almost without pause. But by his Spirit God transforms us, making us content and displaying his power to everyone who sees our lives.

3. *Contentment frees us to serve God and others.* If we are constantly preoccupied with our own situation—the things we lack or the things we wish were different—we won't be looking for opportunities to serve. The most useful people in God's kingdom are those who trust the Lord regardless of outward circumstances.

4. *Contentment keeps us from various temptations to sin.* When we are always thinking about what we would like to change in our circumstances, Satan is quick to respond. He will eagerly tempt us to sinfully demand (or take) the things that God hasn't given us (see Gen. 3:1–5; James 4:1–2). If, instead, we are satisfied with what God has given, we will not give Satan an opportunity in our hearts.

**Reflect:** How are you motivated by reward in your life? What hard things have you been willing to do because of promised gain?

**Reflect:** When have you seen these four blessings of contentment in your life and in the lives of other Christians?

**Act:** Pray and ask God to cultivate contentment in your heart. Ask him to give you the "great gain" he has promised.

# FINDING CONTENTMENT BY LOOKING TO CHRIST

# DAY 4

# Christ, Our Encouragement

*So if there is any encouragement in Christ, any comfort from love, any participation in the Spirit, any affection and sympathy, complete my joy. . . . Do nothing from selfish ambition or conceit, but in humility count others more significant than yourselves. (Phil. 2:1, 3)*

A SEGMENT OF THE BBC documentary series *Human Planet* records the efforts of two fishermen to harvest valuable goose barnacles from the dangerous rocks along Spain's northern coast. The men are attached to each other by a rope, and they take turns descending the cliffs to the water's edge, braving the battering of dangerous waves. As one man gathers barnacles, he depends on the other to watch vigilantly, shouting a warning when a particularly large breaker approaches—and pulling him up to safety if the danger is too great.[1]

Like a fisherman at the bottom of the cliff, we can sometimes feel alone and exposed as we brave the uncomfortable circumstances of our lives. But the reality of the gospel is that we are not alone at all. By his incarnation and life of perfect obedience, by his death and resurrection, Christ has entered in to our human condition and has bound himself to us with cords that cannot be snapped (see Rom. 8:35–39).

As today's verses show us, our union to Christ—the fact that we are "in Christ" (Phil. 2:1)—should bring us encouragement and comfort. He has loved us enough to give himself for us, and he will continue to love us to the end. He has given us his Spirit to help us, and he has showered us with his affection and sympathy. When we are disappointed by the way things have turned out, when we are frustrated by situations that don't seem to change, or when we are baffled by circumstances that change without warning, we do not stand on the cliffs alone but are tethered to Christ.

Our union with Christ also enables us to love others. The rotten fruit of discontent is rivalry and covetousness. Focused on ourselves, we envy the seemingly better circumstances of others. To a discontented heart, our neighbor is not an object of kindness but a symbol of the life we wish we had. But, secure in the eternal love of Christ for us, united to him by faith, and reminded of his sacrifice on our behalf, we can trust him with our circumstances and freely love others.

**Reflect:** How does the knowledge that Christ has bound himself to you and bound you to himself encourage you?

**Reflect:** What are some ways you have wrongly measured your own life against the lives of others? How does knowing that you are eternally secure in Christ's love allow you to love others rather than envying them?

**Act:** Meditate on the Heidelberg Catechism's question "What is your only comfort in life and in death?" and its answer:

That I am not my own, but belong—body and soul, in life and in death—to my faithful Savior, Jesus Christ.

He has fully paid for all my sins with his precious blood, and has set me free from the tyranny of the devil. He also watches over me in such a way that not a hair can fall from my head without the will of my Father in heaven; in fact, all things must work together for my salvation.

Because I belong to him, Christ, by his Holy Spirit, assures me of eternal life and makes me wholeheartedly willing and ready from now on to live for him.[2]

# DAY 5

# Christ, Our Example

*Have this mind among yourselves, which is yours in Christ Jesus,*
*who, though he was in the form of God, did not count equality with*
*God a thing to be grasped, but emptied himself, by taking the form*
*of a servant, being born in the likeness of men. (Phil. 2:5–7)*

DO YOU WANT to know what contentment looks like? Consider the life of a certain man: A king, he became a servant. Self-sufficient, he subjected himself to hunger, thirst, and poverty. Innocent of all wrongdoing, he silently received false accusations and unjust punishment. Never once did this man complain about his circumstances, grumble against the God who gave them, or envy others who had easier lives. Never once did he do anything but trustingly submit to the will of the Father.

When he was alone, he prayed. When he was tempted, he clung to the Word of God. When he was betrayed and disappointed by his friends, he offered forgiveness. Despite the exceptionally difficult circumstances of his own life, this man joyfully and constantly served others. His greatest desire was the glory of God and the eternal good of his neighbor.

This man, of course, is the Lord Jesus.

In today's passage, Paul holds up Christ as an example. Though Christ was eternally God (see v. 6) and deserving of all praise and worship, he willingly took to himself a lowly human nature (see v. 7). In this act of ultimate humility, the king of the universe became a servant.

In our own hearts, pride causes us to shake our fist at providence, thinking that we are better and know better than God. Humility acknowledges that only God knows what is best, and it enables us to receive even his difficult providences with contentment. When Christ became a man, he resisted pride and instead submitted to the Father's will.

Christ, then, is our highest example of contentment. Throughout his life, Christ received the will of the Father with contentment. Perhaps nowhere is this clearer than in his response to his approaching death. In Matthew 26:36–46, Jesus comes before the Father in prayer. He declares his own desire to be spared the horror of the cross, and he pleads with the Father to "let this cup pass" (v. 39). But, ultimately, he freely submits to God's disposal: "not as I will, but as you will" (v. 39). In this, Christ trusts the Father to do what is best even if it means that his own circumstances will be difficult.

As we will see more clearly tomorrow, Christ is not just our example, but is also at work in us by his power to bring us to contentment. The mind of contentment that was his is also "yours in Christ Jesus" (Phil. 2:5).

**Reflect:** You might once have been told, "Do as I say, not as I do." Thankfully, this is not what Christ says to you! Christ never asks you to do something that he himself has not done.

**Reflect:** Read Luke 4:1–13. Satan tempts Jesus to find ultimate satisfaction by changing his circumstances. Material provision, power, and status are areas where we also are tempted to discontent. Notice how Jesus responds to each temptation, and consider how you can follow his example when the Evil One tempts you.

**Act:** Think of a godly person in your life who demonstrates contentment even in difficult circumstances. As you spend time with that person, notice the Christlike habits that he or she practices. If you feel comfortable doing so, ask this person to share what God has taught him or her about contentment over the years.

# DAY 6

## Christ, Our Power

*We know that Christ, being raised from the dead, will never
die again; death no longer has dominion over him. For the
death he died he died to sin, once for all, but the life he lives
he lives to God. So you also must consider yourselves dead to
sin and alive to God in Christ Jesus. (Rom. 6:9–11)*

MULTIPLE STUDIES HAVE demonstrated that time spent on
social media sites makes people feel less happy, more left out, and
increasingly dissatisfied with themselves and their lives. Users'
depression and suicide rates increase, and their feelings of envy
and jealousy correlate directly to their browsing time. Most of us
know this—either from reading the studies or from our own personal experience—and yet we seem powerless to stop scrolling.
Experts tell us that limiting our screen time will provide greater
satisfaction in our lives, but we continue to swipe on.

Simply knowing what habits will curb grumbling and foster contentment doesn't mean that we are able to do them. Pray
more. Watch HGTV less. Memorize Scripture. Stop daydream-
ing. Serve your neighbor. Be thankful. Forget about that missed
promotion. Scripture plainly directs us to turn our eyes "from
looking at worthless things" and instead to meditate on God (see
Ps. 119:36–37). But can we?

The good news of the gospel is not simply that Christ tells us
how to be content but also that Christ is powerfully at work in
us to bring us to contentment. The same Christ who was himself
perfectly content to submit to the Father's will (see Phil. 2:5–8)
is the Christ who—by his Spirit—enables us also to pursue a life
of contentment. As we see in today's verses, our union with him
makes us "dead to sin and alive to God" (Rom. 6:11).

Christ brings us to contentment in a variety of ways. First, his death breaks the power that sin has over us (see Rom. 6:5–14). By uniting us to himself in his death and resurrection, Christ releases us from our slavery to sin and frees us to righteousness. Because of Christ, we do not have to grumble. Christ also brings us to contentment by giving us his indwelling Spirit. The Spirit convicts us of sin and spurs us toward righteousness (see Rom. 8:9–17). Because Christ lives in us, we have ever-present assistance to be holy. Finally, Christ prays for us. The writer to the Hebrews tells us that "he is able to save to the uttermost those who draw near to God through him, since he always lives to make intercession for them" (Heb. 7:25). Just as Christ prayed for Peter before his temptation (see Luke 22:31–32), he is now praying for us to attain contentment.

We do not strive for contentment on our own. At the end of Philippians, Paul writes about contentment: "I can do all things through him who strengthens me" (4:13). Christ has conquered sin, dwells in us by his Spirit, and prays continually for us. We have everything we need.

**Reflect:** What are some habits that would foster contentment in your heart? Do you practice them? Why is it often so hard to do these things? Remind yourself that Christ is the one who works in you and that you are therefore able to pursue holiness.

**Reflect:** Read Hebrews 7:25 and Luke 22:31–32. Meditate on the precious fact that Christ is even now praying for you to gain contentment.

**Act:** When you find yourself tempted to grumble and complain about your circumstances, pray and ask for the help of the Holy Spirit. When you notice a period of contentment, give thanks to the Lord for his powerful work in you.

# DAY 7

# Christ's Glory, Our Goal

*Do all things without grumbling or disputing, that you may*
*be blameless and innocent, children of God without blemish*
*in the midst of a crooked and twisted generation, among*
*whom you shine as lights in the world. (Phil. 2:14–15)*

COMPLAINING IS A universal currency in our world. Almost without fail, it provides a point of connection in even the most casual interactions. Paying at the grocery store? Just grumble about how cold (or hot) the weather has been recently, and you and the checkout clerk will quickly form an alliance. Filling your mug at the office coffee station? Point out how horribly weak (or strong) the brew is today, and your coworkers will vigorously nod their heads in agreement. Late to a party? Mutter about the traffic, and every guest in earshot will have their own gridlock lament to contribute. There is seemingly nothing that we won't complain about, and seemingly no one who won't join us when we do.

But belonging to Christ radically changes everything. Because we know that God does all things for our good and his glory (see Rom. 8:28), because we rest secure in his love for us and our union with him (see Rom. 8:38–39), and because we have been given the indispensable help of his Holy Spirit (see Phil. 2:13), we are not like the murmuring unbelievers around us. We refrain from grumbling, because bringing glory to Christ is our highest goal (see Phil. 2:14–15).

Jesus said, "Let your light shine before others, so that they may see your good works and give glory to your Father who is in heaven" (Matt. 5:16); and, when we refuse to join the office pity-party, we publicly exalt Christ in at least three ways:

1. *We testify that God is good.* Most of us would tell our neighbors that God is good. But our dissatisfied grumblings are a jarring contradiction to what we say we believe. A tongue that is used for both blessing and cursing "ought not to be so" (James 3:10)!
2. *We testify to an unshakeable hope.* When Job's wife encourages him to curse God for the trials in his life, Job replies, "Shall we receive good from God, and shall we not receive evil?" (Job 2:10). By his sinless response, Job testifies that he has faith in God's eternal purposes, whether his outward circumstances appear rosy or grim.
3. *We testify to a deeper reality.* If our conversations with unbelievers are taken up by the minutiae of life's inconveniences, we act like this world is all that matters. Instead, we ought to take every opportunity to point to deeper—and more lasting!—spiritual realities.

**Reflect:** Imagine your typical day minus complaining—no moans about the weather, no groans about the boss or the kids, no sighs about the busyness of your schedule. Which of your interactions or relationships often depend on complaining?

**Reflect:** Read Rev. 19:1–8. When you rejoice in Christ (rather than complaining), you are joining the heavenly multitude in giving glory to God. This is your work in this life, and it will be your glorious task for all eternity.

**Act:** Before you head into a situation in which complaining will likely be the main source of conversation, prepare yourself with something helpful to say instead: Ask the other person a thoughtful question about himself or herself. Express your thankfulness for a blessing. Testify to the goodness of God in the midst of trials.

# CULTIVATING A RIGHT UNDERSTANDING OF MY CIRCUMSTANCES

# DAY 8

# I Have Nothing

*For who sees anything different in you? What do you have*
*that you did not receive? If then you received it, why do*
*you boast as if you did not receive it? (1 Cor. 4:7)*

IN THE OPENING of his *Institutes*, John Calvin writes, "Nearly
all the wisdom we possess, that is to say, true and sound wisdom,
consists of two parts: the knowledge of God and of ourselves."[1]
This is the foundation of contentment, too. For the next few days,
we will turn our attention to meditating on what the Bible says
about ourselves and our circumstances and our God and his
purposes.

First, we must plainly acknowledge that—on our own—we
have nothing and we deserve nothing. This is not a comfortable
truth. We each would like to think that what we have, whether
abilities or relationships or possessions, we have by right or merit.

But the testimony of Scripture is that we were made by God
from dust (see Gen. 2:7) and that everything we have comes from
God. Do you have a family? They are a gift from the Lord (see Ps.
127). Do you work? The tasks of your day were prepared for you
by God (see Eph. 2:10). Did you eat breakfast today? God sup-
plied your daily food (see Matt. 6:11). Is your heart beating? It is
God who gives you each day of your life (see Ps. 139:16).

Even more importantly, all our spiritual blessings are from
God. While we were sinners and rebels against God, he gave his
Son to die on our behalf that we might be reconciled to him (see
Rom. 5:8). In Christ, he gives us every spiritual blessing in the
heavenly places (see Eph. 1:3). What's more, he dwells in us by
his Spirit and cultivates in our hearts the fruit of righteousness
(see Gal. 5:22–26).

A discontented heart denies the graciousness of God, acting as if it had not received everything from God's hand (1 Cor. 4:7) and arrogantly demanding from God as if it deserved something better. This grasping ingratitude has serious consequences, as we see in Romans 1: people who do not "honor him as God or give thanks to him" (v. 21) become "futile in their thinking" (v. 21) and are "filled with all manner of unrighteousness" (v. 29).

But, recognizing our dependence on a gracious God, we can pray with the psalmist, "Bless the LORD, O my soul, and forget not all his benefits, who forgives all your iniquity, who heals all your diseases, who redeems your life from the pit, who crowns you with steadfast love and mercy" (Ps. 103:2–4).

**Reflect:** Look around your home and note the items that were gifts from a friend or family member. What would your home look like if every gift were suddenly removed? Now consider the fact that *everything* you have is a gift from your loving heavenly Father (see James 1:17).

**Reflect:** In Philippians 1:29 Paul says that it has been "granted to you" that "you should not only believe in [Christ] but also suffer for his sake." Do you think of both blessings and trials as being "granted to you" by God?

**Act:** Too often, praying before a meal is a perfunctory ritual with little heart engagement. Today, every time you put food in your mouth or take a drink of water, pause to truly acknowledge your own helpless dependence on God and thank him for his kindness in providing your daily bread.

# DAY 9

# I Can Do Nothing

*Unless the Lord builds the house, those who build it*
*labor in vain. Unless the Lord watches over the city,*
*the watchman stays awake in vain. (Ps. 127:1)*

"She believed she could, so she did."
You probably don't have to travel far from your front door
before you spot this unattributed quote on a T-shirt or tattoo. The
sentiment is nothing new, of course. Ever since the engineers at
Babel first drew up their blueprints (see Gen. 11:1–9), men and
women have always believed that they can do anything they set
their minds—or hearts—on accomplishing.

But consider the truth of Psalm 127: "Unless the Lord builds
the house, those who build it labor in vain. Unless the Lord
watches over the city, the watchman stays awake in vain. It is in
vain that you rise up early and go late to rest, eating the bread of
anxious toil; for he gives to his beloved sleep" (v. 1–2). No matter
how determined or hardworking we are, we depend entirely on
the Lord to establish the work of our hands. Even the seemingly
passive activity of a good night's sleep is a gift from the Lord!

Spiritually, we can't do anything for ourselves either. We were
dead in sin; God made us alive (see Col. 2:13). We were rebels;
God made us his friends (see Rom. 5:10). We were blind; God
gave us eyes to see his glory (see 2 Cor. 4:4–6). We were ignorant;
God revealed himself to us (see Isa. 9:2). We were slaves to Satan;
God redeemed us for himself and made us his heirs (see Titus
3:3–7). We have been saved, "not because of works done by us in
righteousness, but according to [God's] own mercy" (Titus 3:5).

We are often discontented because we believe the lie of
autonomy. We tell ourselves that if we do certain things—such as

work hard or create opportunities for ourselves—we will accomplish what we intend. And then, when we are unable to do what we want or fail to reach the goal we have in mind, we become frustrated.

When we act like we are almighty, we will be disappointed every time. Like the Israelites who insisted on trusting in their own power, we need to hear the reminder of Isaiah: "For thus said the Lord GOD, the Holy One of Israel, 'In returning and rest you shall be saved; in quietness and in trust shall be your strength'" (30:15).

**Reflect:** When you were a child, you probably read *The Little Engine That Could* or another story about accomplishing a goal through willpower and hard work. Why do you think such stories are appealing? Why are they misleading?

**Reflect:** Read God's words to Job in Job 38–41. Allow yourself to be humbled in the presence of your God—"Have you an arm like God, and can you thunder with a voice like his?" (40:9)—and then make Job's response your own: "I know that you can do all things, and that no purpose of yours can be thwarted" (42:2).

**Act:** This morning, commit your day to the Lord with an honest acknowledgment of your own weakness and a sincere request for his sustaining grace in every moment.

# DAY 10

# God Takes Discontent Seriously

*We must not put Christ to the test, as some of them did and were destroyed by serpents, nor grumble, as some of them did and were destroyed by the Destroyer. Now these things happened to them as an example, but they were written down for our instruction, on whom the end of the ages has come. (1 Cor. 10:9–11)*

MANY OF GOD's judgments recorded in the Bible can seem shockingly drastic. Miriam contracted leprosy after opposing Moses (see Num. 12:1–10). Uzzah died on the spot after trying to keep the ark of the covenant from toppling (see 2 Sam. 6:5–8). Ananias and Sapphira died after lying about how much money they had put in the offering plate (see Acts 5:1–11). Some Corinthian Christians became terminally ill after taking the Lord's Supper thoughtlessly (see 1 Cor. 11:27–30).

While we may be tempted to think that those sins were not a big deal, God's righteous response demonstrates that they were extremely serious. Our recoil at the consequences should cause us to take a closer look at our own hearts (see 1 Cor. 10:9–11).

Today's passage reveals the deep sinfulness of grumbling. Having been rescued by God from slavery in Egypt, the Israelites proceeded to complain. They grumbled about the drinking water (see Ex. 15:24; 17:3), about the food (see Ex. 16:2–3), and about Moses's judgment of Korah (see Num. 16:41). They complained about "their misfortunes" (Num. 11:1) and murmured when they were afraid of their enemies (see Deut. 1:27). Perhaps most significantly, the whole assembly grumbled after they heard the faithless report of the ten spies (see Num. 14:2). With complete sincerity, they demanded to be taken back to the land of their slavery (see Num. 14:3–4).

And so God judged them for their sin by refusing to allow them to enter the land of promise (see Num. 14:28–35). Because they grumbled, God declared to them, "Your dead bodies shall fall in this wilderness" (v. 29). Because they grumbled, they all died.

What makes discontent so serious? Consider three things:

1. *Discontent is rebellion against God.* When we complain about the things God has done or the things he has withheld, we accuse him of acting wrongly.
2. *Discontent keeps us from love for God.* If we believe that God has acted wrongly, we will not serve and love him with heart, soul, mind, and strength (see Mark 12:30).
3. *Discontent leads to other sins.* Idolatry, selfishness, anger, covetousness, slander, stealing, adultery, and even murder often begin as discontent (see, for example, Rom. 1:21–32; James 4:1–3).

**Reflect:** What sins do you think of as particularly serious? What sins do you tend to minimize as not that significant? How do you typically categorize grumbling and discontent?

**Reflect:** Read Numbers 13–14. Notice how the fear and anxiety of the ten spies stirs up the whole community to widespread grumbling against the Lord. Contrast this with the faith of Joshua and Caleb that manifests as quiet contentment.

**Act:** Every time you find yourself complaining today, consider that this sin merits your destruction. Repent. Then meditate with thankfulness on the words of Isaiah about the Lord Jesus: "He was pierced for our transgressions; he was crushed for our iniquities; upon him was the chastisement that brought us peace, and with his wounds we are healed" (53:5).

# God's Care for Me Is More Certain Than Life's Changing Circumstances

*Keep your life free from love of money, and be content with what you have, for he has said, "I will never leave you nor forsake you." So we can confidently say, "The Lord is my helper; I will not fear; what can man do to me?" (Heb. 13:5–6)*

SOMEONE ONCE ASKED American industrialist and philanthropist John D. Rockefeller, "How much money is enough?" He reportedly replied, "Just a little bit more."[1] In his day, Rockefeller was the richest man in the world, but his comment reveals something about money that everyone—rich or poor—ought to remember: money is unreliable. What seems like enough money in the morning will not be enough when the stock market report comes out in the evening. What seems like enough money on Monday will not be enough when the bills arrive on Friday. What seems like enough money this year will not be enough when you have a medical emergency or a major home repair or an unexpected pregnancy next year.

No matter whether your bank account balance shows seven digits or only one, riches will always be an unreliable hope (see 1 Tim. 6:17). Thankfully, in today's passage the writer to the Hebrews reminds us that, though money is uncertain, God's care for us is always certain.

In addition to money, this entire life is full of areas of uncertainty, and the Bible tells us it is good for us to acknowledge our fleeting condition: "O LORD, make me know my end and what is the measure of my days; let me know how fleeting I am!" (Ps. 39:4).

Why does the psalmist want God to remind him of the frailty of human existence? Because, as he writes a few verses later, "And now, O Lord, for what do I wait? My hope is in you" (Ps. 39:7). Having acknowledged that everything else in life is unreliable, we can rest in the certainty of God's care.

This is also the message of Hebrews 13:5–6. The secret of contentment is not in having "enough" money (or status or relationships or education). Rather, the secret of contentment is placing our ultimate hope in something secure: The Lord will never leave us or forsake us; he is our help, so there is no reason to fear. The God who has loved us with an everlasting love (see Jer. 31:3) will continue to care for us through all the changing circumstances of our fleeting lives.

> **Reflect:** How much money do you think is "enough"? What other unreliable things do you often strive to get "enough" of (e.g., relationships, knowledge, power, recognition, and so on)? Think of a time when you were frustrated because you had set your hope on an unreliable goal.
>
> **Reflect:** Meditate on the words of this hymn by John Newton: "Fading is the worldling's pleasure, all his boasted pomp and show; solid joys and lasting treasure none but Zion's children know."[2] Pray and ask God to remind you of your frailty and to give you confidence in his certain care.
>
> **Act:** Memorize Psalm 73:26: "My flesh and my heart may fail, but God is the strength of my heart and my portion forever."

# DAY 12

# The Circumstances of My Life Are Carefully Designed for the Good of My Undying Soul

*In this you rejoice, though now for a little while, if necessary, you
have been grieved by various trials, so that the tested genuineness
of your faith—more precious than gold that perishes though it
is tested by fire—may be found to result in praise and glory and
honor at the revelation of Jesus Christ. (1 Peter 1:6–7)*

PROBABLY SOMEWHERE IN your home you have a toolbox.
It may be a small kit with just a few essentials—a hammer, two
screwdrivers, and a wrench—or it may be a large, multi-drawer
case containing a dozen hand tools plus hundreds of different
drill bits, sockets, and hex keys. The extent of your tool kit is usually an indication of the use that you have for it. Some of us limit
ourselves to hanging a picture or two and tightening the occasional loose screw; we can make do with a scant handful of tools.
Others depend on their massive collection of tools for everything
from furniture construction to major car repairs.

Today's verses show us that God is doing a precise and priceless task—and has an extensive set of tools at his disposal. Long
before you were aware of it, God has been at work to make you
"conformed to the image of his Son" (Rom. 8:29). Your holiness
is the reason that Christ died (see Col. 1:22), and your holiness is
the "praise of his glory" (Eph. 1:12, 14).

Everything that happens in your life, then, is designed by
God to make you more like Christ (see Rom. 8:28–30). The trials of your life, as well as the blessings, are God's carefully cali-
brated tools to accomplish his work in you. Though difficult

41

times may feel like an indiscriminate blow from a sledgehammer, we have God's assurance that they are precisely what is "necessary" (1 Peter 1:6). And though our trials may feel like they will never end, we have his word that they are only "for a little while" (1 Pet. 1:6). When a particular trial threatens to overwhelm you, remember that God has already lovingly determined the precise moment when your difficulty will end.[1]

At first glance, it is surprising that Peter calls us to "rejoice" in these various trials (1 Peter 1:6). When we face broken relationships, financial stress, or physical illness, most of us do not naturally greet these hardships with joy! But our contentment rests in the fact that God is using those things to do a priceless work in our souls—something much more lasting than even gold.

**Reflect:** A painter needs high-quality paintbrushes, a software engineer needs a powerful computer, a baker needs a commercial oven. What is something you do that requires precise tools? In what way are the circumstances of your life tools in the hand of God?

**Reflect:** Read about the life of Joseph in Genesis 37 and 39–41. Then read his perspective on his many trials in Gen. 45:1–15. Are you able to say with Joseph about your trials, "You meant evil against me, but God meant it for good" (Gen. 50:20)?

**Act:** Make a list of trials that are currently grieving you. Bring that list before the Lord in prayer. Acknowledge that, though these things are not easy, you trust him that they are necessary (see 1 Peter 1:6). Ask him to use each one to reveal "the tested genuineness of your faith" (1 Peter 1:7). Thank him for the privilege of participating in the "praise and glory and honor" of Jesus Christ (1 Peter 1:7).

# CULTIVATING
# RIGHT DESIRES

# DAY 13

# Desire Must Be Trained

*Incline my heart to your testimonies, and not to selfish gain! Turn my eyes from looking at worthless things; and give me life in your ways. (Ps. 119:36–37)*

IF YOU WANT to change the way you eat, most diet plans recommend that you clear the junk food and sweets from your pantry shelves and replace those items with healthier options. That way, when you get hungry, you will find yourself standing in front of a refrigerator full of fruits and veggies rather than an entire cheesecake. Hopefully, if you consistently eat nutritious foods, you will develop new eating habits, and those nightly cravings for a bowl of cookie dough ice cream will diminish or disappear.

When it comes to diet, we generally understand that we don't always want what is good for us and that we will probably have to do some work to train our desires in a better direction. What's true of our food preferences is also true of the rest of our desires. Whether it's our financial goals, our sexual appetites, our beauty aspirations, or our educational ambitions, we don't always desire the right things in the right way to the right degree.

The Bible never proposes that we arrive at contentment by refusing to have any desires. In fact, desire is central to the Christian life. Right desire fuels prayer, motivates obedience, and unifies believers. Just as changing our eating habits doesn't mean we must stop ever being hungry, pursuing contentment doesn't require us to avoid desire completely. As Melissa Kruger writes in *The Envy of Eve*, "Our goal is not to stop our longings altogether, but to refine our desires and align them with the Lord's will for our lives."[1]

To start, like a nutritionist clearing the candy from our cabinets, the Lord plainly tells us what kinds of desires we must avoid:

- a desire for anything that God says in his Word is sinful: for example, having sex outside marriage
- a desire that leads to sin: for example, wanting something so much that you steal it
- any "inordinate"[2] desire (a desire that is sinfully out of proportion): for example, focusing so much on your appearance that you neglect your soul

God's Word also tells us what we *ought* to desire and sets priorities for those desires. We will be looking at this further in the next few days.

As we seek a contented heart, we must ask the Lord to grant us the grace of rightly ordered desires: "Incline my heart to your testimonies, and not to selfish gain! Turn my eyes from looking at worthless things; and give me life in your ways" (Ps. 119:36–37).

**Reflect:** In our culture, desire is sacrosanct. To tell people that they want the wrong thing is seen as intolerant and unjust. How have you seen this prevailing philosophy expressed? How do you think that you may have been influenced by it?

**Reflect:** Read Jeremiah 17:9: "The heart is deceitful above all things, and desperately sick; who can understand it?" Do you think of your desires as the products of a "deceitful" and "sick" heart?

**Act:** As you go through your day, examine the things that you desire. Consider both the small things (your selection at the drive-through) and the bigger things (your hope for a pay raise). Do you fail to desire the right things in the right way to the right degree?

# DAY 14

# God Sets the Priorities
# for My Desires

*"Therefore do not be anxious, saying, 'What shall we eat?' or 'What shall we drink?' or 'What shall we wear?' For the Gentiles seek after all these things, and your heavenly Father knows that you need them all. But seek first the kingdom of God and his righteousness, and all these things will be added to you." (Matt. 6:31–33)*

WHY DO WE want what we want? Every day, we make dozens of choices about what to watch, who to spend time with, where to spend our paychecks, and when to eat dinner. One study estimates that we make over two hundred choices a day simply about food![1] These choices are motivated by our desires. And our desires, as Louis Menard writes in *The New Yorker*, are shaped by a myriad of factors: "Some combination of inputs including, but not limited to, reasons, hunches, bodily needs, past experiences, unconscious desires, social pressures, mystic chords of memory, and price point is behind every preference; they are weighted differently in almost every case; and they are highly malleable."[2]

As we discussed yesterday, desire is central to our Christian life. And we must allow our "highly malleable" desires to be shaped by the God who made us and sustains us. God, in his Word, tells us what we shouldn't desire, and God, in his Word, sets the priorities for what we ought to desire. As we will see today, we arrive at contentment when we match our desires to the desires of God himself.

In our passage, Jesus graciously reorients our priorities, turning our focus away from ourselves. He reminds us that the worthiest objects of our desire are not always the ones right in front of our face. It is easy to wake up every morning consumed with material and bodily concerns: the dwindling bank account, the leaking roof, the looming health diagnosis. It takes more work— *seeking* (see v. 33)—to be first consumed with the unseen things that God calls most important: the cause of missions, the purity of the church, the state of your own soul. But this is exactly the priority God sets for us.

How, then, can we move those other desires down on our list? How can we be content when the roof is still leaking and the kids still need new backpacks? How can we pray for the spread of the gospel when the cancer is spreading deep in our own bones? Jesus tells us two precious truths: God knows exactly what we need (see v. 32), and God has the power to satisfy every righteous desire (see v. 33).

Desires that are trained by God himself, ordered according to his priorities, and pursued in submission to his will are good. These are also the desires that will certainly be satisfied—whether in this life or in eternity. And in that, we can rest content.

**Reflect:** What factors influence your desires? How often do you consider God's priorities when setting your own?

**Reflect:** Read Psalm 37:4: "Delight yourself in the LORD, and he will give you the desires of your heart." Notice how the psalmist finds contentment by matching his desires to the will of the Lord.

**Act:** Use the prayer the Lord taught to his disciples (see Matt. 6:9–13) as the model for your own prayer today. Allow your personal desires to be trained by God's priorities. Be satisfied whenever you see one of these requests being answered. Be encouraged that God will surely fulfill all these desires— whether now or in eternity.

# DAY 15

# Desiring God's Glory

*"Pray then like this: Our Father in heaven, hallowed be your name. Your kingdom come, your will be done, on earth as it is in heaven." (Matt. 6:9–10)*

ATTEND ANY MAJOR sporting event, and you will find your-self surrounded by enthusiastic fans. They'll be wearing the team colors and holding hand-painted signs. During breaks in the game, they will heartily sing the team fight song from memory. And, play by play, they'll intently follow the action below. When, at the final buzzer, the home team clinches the victory, you'll hear the fans shout to one another, "We won!"

In the world of sports, people who never even touched the ball joyfully declare themselves to be winners and go home satisfied.

Likewise, as Christians, our desires are so bound up with God's glory that a victory for our Lord is a victory in which we have a share. In today's passage, Jesus directs the desires of his followers by teaching them how to pray. Prayer, as the Westminster Shorter Catechism defines it, is "an offering up of our desires unto God,"[1] and so Jesus's model prayer is instruction about what we should want and how badly we should want it.

Today and tomorrow, we will look at the prayer that we commonly call "The Lord's Prayer." In it there are six different petitions that the Lord teaches us to ask, and today we see that the first three petitions are for the Lord to be honored in the hearts of people. Jesus here teaches us that, before we have any concern for ourselves, we ought to be jealous for the name of the Lord. We ask God to "hallow" his name (see v. 9)—to make himself known and worshipped in all places at all times. And we ask God to cause his will to be done (see v. 10)—to bring people to serve and love him.

Why is it that we find contentment in seeking God's glory rather than our own personal desires? It is because, as children of the heavenly Father, we have a share in his glory (see Rom. 8:17). Jeremiah Burroughs explains it this way: "If God has glory, I have glory; God's glory is my glory, and therefore God's will is mine; if God has riches, then I have riches; if God is magnified, then I am magnified; if God is satisfied, then I am satisfied."[2]

Our desires for God's glory will be satisfied! God will certainly be exalted both now and for all eternity—when "every knee shall bow" and "every tongue shall confess" (Rom. 14:11) and a "great multitude that no one [can] number" will sing his praises and never cease (Rev. 7:9).

**Reflect:** Think about the typical subjects of your prayers. What things do you pray for often? What things do you rarely pray for? What do your prayers reveal about what you really desire?

**Reflect:** In today's passage, Jesus teaches us to pray to God as "Our Father." When we remember that God is not a distant deity but is, in fact, our dear Father, we earnestly desire his glory. Just as earthly children delight when their dad is praised by others, we experience great joy when our heavenly Father is honored.

**Act:** Notice the ways all around you that God is glorified: shining stars (see Ps. 19:1), singing children (see Ps. 8:2), a welcoming church (see Rom. 15:7), professing Christians (see Phil. 2:11). Rejoice in those things, knowing that God's glory is your glory and that when the God whom you love is satisfied, you can be satisfied too.

# DAY 16

# Desiring Daily Provision
# from God's Hand

*"Give us this day our daily bread." (Matt. 6:11)*

MOST OF US can think of someone from our childhood who loved to feed us. A grandmother who always pulled cookies out of the oven at the moment of our arrival. A dad who splurged on hot dogs and soda at the baseball game. A neighbor who poured paper cups of cold juice, a friend who shared the sandwich from her lunch box, a teacher who rewarded a year of good behavior with pizza and ice cream sundaes. These people seemed to enjoy nothing more than watching us arrive hungry and leave satisfied.

So far in our study of contentment we have set our desires on the highest priorities that God sets for us: the big, glorious, eternal purposes of his glory and his will. But we must not think that God is indifferent toward our physical and material needs. Today's passage, the fourth petition of the Lord's Prayer, shows us that God is also concerned about the most basic needs of his children. Our God loves to see us arrive hungry and leave satisfied.

We cannot overestimate the care that the Lord has for our bodies and our earthly circumstances. The one who knit our bodies together in the womb remembers that we are dust (see Pss. 103:14; 139:13). Out of his great love for us, he tenderly clothes, heals, prospers, and feeds us (Ps. 90:17; Matt. 6:26, 30; James 5:15). He numbers our days, the hairs of our heads, and every tear that falls from our eyes (see Pss. 56:8; 139:16; Matt. 10:30). It shouldn't be a surprise, then, that he wants us to ask him for our material needs.

But what does it mean to pray for "daily bread"? The *First*

*Catechism* explains the petition this way: "We are asking God to provide us with all that we really need."[1] If we are honest with ourselves, we can acknowledge that we don't always correctly understand what we really need. The must-have toys of childhood give way to the must-have gadgets and relationships and job opportunities of adulthood. The things that we think we need tonight are revealed as passing fancies in the morning. But when we pray "Give us this day our daily bread," we are asking the all-wise God who knows and loves us to give us exactly what is best.

Notice the tender kindness of the Lord expressed in Matthew 6:26: "Look at the birds of the air: they neither sow nor reap nor gather into barns, and yet your heavenly Father feeds them. Are you not of more value than they?" We do not hesitate to bring our physical and material desires to God. In fact, he commands us to ask for them! We can boldly ask for pay raises and marriage proposals and clean bills of health. But, as we pray, we rest content that God alone knows—and provides—what we really need.

**Reflect:** What is something that you once thought was a "need" but later realized was merely a personal desire?

**Reflect:** Read Exodus 16, and consider the Lord's provision for the Israelites in the wilderness. What did God's people assume that they needed (v. 3)? What did God provide instead? When did they gather manna? How much did they need? What do you think the Israelites learned from waiting for manna every day for forty years?

**Act:** Bring your material desires before the Lord in prayer, trusting him to give you "all that you really need," whatever that might be.

# DAY 17

# Desiring Holiness

*As obedient children, do not be conformed to the passions*
*of your former ignorance, but as he who called you is holy,*
*you also be holy in all your conduct, since it is written, "You*
*shall be holy, for I am holy." (1 Peter 1:14–16)*

IN 1521, POWERFUL AND ANGRY church authorities
assembled at the Diet of Worms and demanded that German
reformer Martin Luther retract his teachings. Though his life was
in the balance, Luther courageously answered, "My conscience is
captive to the Word of God. I cannot and I will not retract anything, since it is neither safe nor right to go against conscience."[1]

How was it possible for Luther to stand resolutely unmoved
in the face of extremely trying circumstances? As his answer to
the church authorities shows, it was because he valued pleasing God more than he valued anything else. For Luther, facing
an almost certain death sentence with a clear conscience was far
safer than wandering into sin.

In today's verse, we see that one of our highest desires ought
to be a life of holiness—a holiness so complete that Peter com-
pares it to the holiness of God himself (see v. 15). God is the one
who sets us apart from the "passions of . . . ignorance" (v. 14) all
around us, and so God is the one who we seek to imitate. The Lord
urges us to "walk in a manner worthy of the Lord, fully pleasing
to him: bearing fruit in every good work and increasing in the
knowledge of God" (Col. 1:10; see also Eph. 4:1; 1 Thess. 2:12).
Christ died for us and lives in us, and so we want to please him.

And when we stand on obedience to God's Word, hating and
forsaking sin wherever we find it, we will grow in contentment.
William Barcley writes, "If sin is our greatest burden, all other

burdens are made lighter."[2] When we are faced with temptations to be discontent—when our plans fall through and the rain clouds mount on the horizon—we should make holiness our first concern. Whatever our circumstances, no matter how disappointing, the thought of disappointing our God should be even more pressing. When we make holiness one of our greatest desires, every circumstance becomes an opportunity to practice obedience.

Holiness is a constant struggle, and we will not be perfectly holy until the last day (see 1 John 3:2). But we do not fight sin alone. At great cost to himself, Christ secured our forgiveness and freed us from sin's guilt and power. By his Spirit, he puts sin to death in our hearts and brings forth the fruit of righteousness. Encouraged by his work in us, we can pray the prayer of nineteenth-century Presbyterian minister Robert Murray M'Cheyne: "Lord, make me as holy as a pardoned sinner can be."[3]

**Reflect:** Think of a time when you responded sinfully to unfavorable circumstances. You may have grumbled about an unfulfilled goal or envied someone whose situation looked more appealing. How would your response have been different if you had valued your own holiness more?

**Reflect:** Read Philippians 2:12–13: "As you have always obeyed . . . work out your own salvation with fear and trembling, for it is God who works in you, both to will and to work for his good pleasure." We pursue holiness, but we are not muscling through on our own. God is at work to make us holy.

**Act:** The next time you are tempted to grumble about your circumstances, consider the high value that God places on your holiness. In fact, he prizes it so much that he sent his Son to die for it. Ask God to help you prioritize holiness no matter your situation.

# DAY 18

# Righteous Discontent

*Whom have I in heaven but you? And there is nothing on earth that I desire besides you. My flesh and my heart may fail, but God is the strength of my heart and my portion forever. (Ps. 73:25–26)*

NINETEENTH-CENTURY AUTHOR and hymn writer Elizabeth Payson Prentiss lived a life of exemplary faith in the midst of serious trials. For most of her life, she was confined to bed as an invalid, and her husband also suffered from ill health. In 1852, over a period of three months, their two young children died. Later she wrote in a letter, "To love Christ more—this is the deepest need, the constant cry of my soul. Down in the bowling-alley, and out in the woods, and on my bed, and out driving, when I am happy and busy, and when I am sad and idle, the whisper keeps going up for more love, more love, more love!"[1]

Today, as we come to the end of our mediations on right desires, we will see that our highest desire in all of life is to know and love our Lord more. In fact, the psalmist in today's passage is so intent on seeking God that he calls it his *only* desire: "There is nothing on earth that I desire besides you" (v. 25). He isn't saying, of course, that there is literally nothing else he desires. He is saying that, by comparison, every other desire seems like nothing.

The psalmist's prayer highlights what we might call "godly discontent."[2] Because we live in a fallen world and are not yet arrived at our eternal home, we will necessarily—and rightly—be discontent in some areas. For example, we *should* be discontent with:

- *Our sin.* Until the day of Christ's return, when we are made perfect in holiness, we will always be dissatisfied with our own sinful actions. Paul voices this godly discontent in Romans 7: "For I do not do the good I want, but the evil I do not want is what I keep on doing" (v. 19).

- *Wickedness in the world.* It is right for us to be frustrated when ungodliness abounds. As the psalmist writes, "My eyes shed streams of tears, because people do not keep your law" (Ps. 119:136).
- *Our knowledge of God.* As we see in today's verses, our quest to know more of God is an ongoing one. Like the psalmist in another passage, we rightly acknowledge, "Great is the LORD, and greatly to be praised, and his greatness is unsearchable" (Ps. 145:3).

It might seem contradictory to say that we are to be content and discontent at the same time, but the Bible holds both to be true. Like the heroes of the faith in Hebrews 11, we are those who don't always have our right desires satisfied in this life, but who are "looking forward to the city that has foundations, whose designer and builder is God" (v. 10).

**Reflect:** Have you ever thought to yourself, "I would be satisfied if only ____"? What does your answer reveal about your deepest desires?

**Reflect:** Jeremiah Burroughs writes that a Christian is "the most contented man in the world, and yet the most unsatisfied man in the world."[3] How would you explain this? In what ways are you content? In what ways are you rightly unsatisfied? Read Hebrews 11.

**Act:** As you face a disappointing or trying circumstance today, make Elizabeth Prentiss's prayer of godly discontent your own: "More love, more love, more love!"

# CULTIVATING A
# THANKFUL HEART

# DAY 19

# Thanksgiving Is God's Will for Me

*Rejoice always, pray without ceasing, give thanks
in all circumstances; for this is the will of God
in Christ Jesus for you. (1 Thess. 5:16–18)*

ON THE FOURTH Thursday of November, Americans celebrate Thanksgiving Day. Officially established as an annual observance by President Abraham Lincoln in 1863, the day has become a major holiday—marked by family, feasting, football, and a televised parade featuring giant helium balloons. Sadly, the practice of thanksgiving is often momentary and superficial, if it even happens at all.

But for Christians, thanksgiving is not merely incidental. It is central to our lives. In today's passage, Paul exhorts us to "give thanks in all circumstances," telling us that "this is the will of God" for us (v. 18). The Bible calls us to give thanks at all times (see Ps. 34:1), in all places (see Ps. 48:10), and from one generation to the next (see Ps. 79:13). Thanksgiving will also be the work of eternity—we will join the heavenly company in an unceasing hymn of thanksgiving (see Rev. 4:8–11; 11:16–18; 19:6–8).

Biblical thanksgiving is not false cheer slapped on the surface of otherwise bad circumstances. Biblical thanksgiving is our acknowledgment that God is accomplishing his eternal purposes, even when we cannot clearly see what he is doing. We "give thanks in all circumstances" because we trust that those very circumstances come from the powerful and gracious hand of our covenant-making and covenant-keeping God.

By contrast, the Bible strongly warns us against ingratitude. In Romans 1, we read a sobering description of the ungodly: "For although they knew God, they did not honor him as God or give thanks to him" (v. 21). Thanksgiving is central to the Christian life; ingratitude is entirely contrary to it.

Unexpected and unwelcome circumstances—a job loss, a fractured bone, a bruised relationship—often leave us feeling uncertain, frantically wondering what we should do next. But our steps are not as unclear as we often assume. God's will for us in all circumstances is thanksgiving. Without hesitation, we can thank him for his sovereign care and gracious purpose in all the details of our lives, accepting from his hand even the difficulties of the present moment.

And in the act of giving thanks, we will find contentment for whatever happens next: "When thanksgiving is understood as establishing the fact that God is a powerful and faithful God who can and will fulfill his promises, thanksgiving becomes the basis for trusting God in the face of an uncertain future."[1]

**Reflect:** What recent, unexpected event has left you feeling shaken? When you encounter such circumstances, do you ever find yourself anxiously wondering what you should do next? Take comfort from the simple truth of today's verse: "give thanks in all circumstances; for this is the will of God in Christ Jesus for you" (v. 18).

**Reflect:** Read Acts 16:16–40. When Paul and Silas were unjustly imprisoned, how did they respond (see v. 25)? What were the effects of their obedient thanksgiving (see vv. 29–34)?

**Act:** Use the minor frustrations of your day as opportunities to practice giving thanks to God. Rain on your picnic? Give thanks to the God who sends the clouds to water the earth (see Job 5:10). Traffic on your commute? Give thanks to the God who establishes your way (see Prov. 16:9). Sinus headache on your day off? Give thanks to the God who made you and takes cares of you (see Ps. 139:1–6).

# DAY 20

# Giving Thanks for Salvation

*For a day in your courts is better than a thousand elsewhere.*
*I would rather be a doorkeeper in the house of my God*
*than dwell in the tents of wickedness. (Ps. 84:10)*

IF YOU HAVE ever been sick, even for just a few days, you know how good it feels to get better. When the cold or flu or stomach bug recedes, the simplest aspects of your normal life suddenly seem extraordinarily wonderful. A five-minute walk in the sunshine is like an exotic vacation. A steaming bowl of chicken soup tastes like a gourmet feast. Even the act of taking a shower and getting dressed is luxurious—simply because you are not sick anymore.

Once upon a time, our spiritual situation was likewise bleak. In fact, we were dead. "You were dead in the trespasses and sins in which you once walked, following the course of this world, following the prince of the power of the air . . . and were by nature children of wrath, like the rest of mankind" (Eph. 2:1–3). Like the patient confined to her bed, we were both helpless and hopeless.

And then, everything changed. "But God, being rich in mercy . . . made us alive together with Christ—by grace you have been saved" (Eph. 2:4–5). Because of the work of Christ on our behalf—his life of perfect obedience, his death on the cross, his resurrection and ascension—we are no longer dead. We are wonderfully alive!

The single fact of our rescue from the justly deserved wrath of God changes how we see everything. We now hate the things that were part of our old life. We no longer find pleasure in the sin and ignorance that once characterized our days. Instead, we delight in every aspect of our new life in Christ. Now we can pray. We can sing songs of praise. We can hear God speak to us through his Word. We can fellowship with everyone else who is likewise united to him. As theologian J. Todd Billings explains, "We . . . enter into the playful, joyous world of *living as children of a gracious Father, as persons united to Christ and empowered by the Spirit*."[1] What could be more wonderful?

Like the psalmist in today's verse, we rejoice in a "day" in the Lord's fellowship, and we count it "better than a thousand elsewhere." We never stop giving thanks for our salvation, because we who belong to Christ are rich indeed.

**Reflect:** Think of a time when someone rescued you from a potentially dangerous situation. Maybe someone caught you as you were falling or shouted a warning about a speeding car. How did you feel toward that person when you realized how close you had come to catastrophe? What did you say to them?

**Reflect:** Read Psalm 136, the Israelites' song of thanksgiving for their deliverance from slavery in Egypt. Notice how each verse savors a different aspect of their salvation. Use this psalm as a model to meditate on the steadfast love of God toward you.

**Act:** Choose a favorite hymn about the saving work of Christ on your behalf (such as "Amazing Grace" or "In Christ Alone.") If you don't already have it memorized, find a copy of the lyrics or play a recording. Sing the words with thanksgiving in your heart.

# DAY 21

# Giving Thanks for Daily Provision

*And day by day, attending the temple together and breaking bread in their homes, they received their food with glad and generous hearts, praising God and having favor with all the people. (Acts 2:46–47)*

IN 1918, ERIC ENSTROM took a photograph he called "Grace," and, ever since, oil-paint reproductions of the iconic print have hung in countless Christian homes and churches. In the image, a white-bearded, elderly man bows his head in prayer over a simple meal of gruel and bread. Enstrom later said, "I wanted to take a picture that would show people that even though they had to do without many things because of the war they still had much to be thankful for."[1]

Enstrom's photograph captures a familiar moment. Whether our menu includes a bowl of cereal or steak and potatoes, whether we are alone or eating with a group, whether we fold our hands or join them with others, Christians "say grace" multiple times every day. And though this is our habit, it is far from meaningless. In fact, the practice of sincerely thanking God for meeting our daily needs may be one of our most important spiritual disciplines.

This was certainly the practice of the members of the early church—who, as we see in today's verses, "received their food with glad and generous hearts" (v. 46). Jesus also prayed before his beach meal with his disciples (see Luke 24:30), and Paul prayed before his shipboard meal with two hundred sailors (see Acts 27:35–37). Our daily provision is not something we can supply for ourselves, and we ought to make a habit of giving thanks to God.

Daily provision is more than just food, of course. If you have a heart that continues to beat and lungs that continue to breathe, you have received gracious, life-sustaining gifts from the Lord. If you have a measure of safety today, if you have friends or family to provide companionship, if you have somewhere to sleep tonight, if you have work to do in your home or church or community, you have those things because the Lord has given them to you.

And it is in our unchanging God that our contentment lies. "Every good gift and every perfect gift," James reminds us, "is from above, coming down from the Father of lights, with whom there is no variation or shadow due to change" (James 1:17). As we saw on day 16, we can be confident that the Lord faithfully gives us "all that we really need"[2]—and for that we should be thankful.

**Reflect:** Our prayers of thanksgiving before meals are often rushed and perfunctory. Sometimes we neglect them altogether. What prevents you from making mealtime prayer a heartfelt expression of thanks to God?

**Reflect:** Read Genesis 2. Notice the tender care that God showed in making the world an ideal place for human life. For the good of people, God created trees as a source of beauty and food (see v. 9), he established meaningful work (see v. 15), and he provided companionship (see v. 18). Thanks be to God!

**Act:** The next time you go to the grocery store or farmers' market, take a moment to look around you. Notice the variety of fruits and vegetables, the abundance of breads, and the selection of fish and meat. Give thanks to the Lord for the cornucopia of foods that daily nourish you.

# Giving Thanks for God's Purposes

*Delight yourself in the LORD, and he will give you
the desires of your heart. (Ps. 37:4)*

IN 1944, BETSIE TEN BOOM and her family were arrested by Nazi soldiers for hiding Jews in their home. Arriving at Ravensbruck concentration camp, she and her sister Corrie entered their barracks to a putrid smell and a biting swarm of fleas. Immediately—and to Corrie's amazement—Betsie began to thank God for everything in the filthy room, including the fleas.

In the following days, the sisters held nightly Bible studies with the women in their dorm. Though the camp was heavily patrolled by police, their meetings were never interrupted. Months later, they discovered why. The unwelcome swarm of fleas, the subject of Betsie's unlikely thanksgiving, had protected the sisters from discovery and enabled hundreds of women to hear the gospel of Christ.[1]

Betsie ten Boom didn't love fleas. What she loved was the purpose of the Lord—and she trusted him that, if he gave swarms of fleas, they must serve some good part of his gracious plan. Her thanksgiving for the fleas was an act of faith and an expression of her heart's true desire.

In today's verse, the psalmist teaches us that when our hearts are set on God's purposes, we will always find those desires fulfilled. The Lord has laid out for us in Scripture many of his plans, including: to exalt Christ (Phil. 2:9–11); to save sinners (John 3:16); to give his people the Holy Spirit (Luke 11:11–13); to establish and protect his church (Matt. 16:18); to make his people holy (Eph. 1:4); to expand his kingdom (Isa. 9:7).

Like Betsie ten Boom, we have an opportunity to give

thanks for these good purposes, even when our circumstances seem unpleasant or uncertain. Though we may not immediately understand the value of fleas or financial failure, we trust that God is completing his good work in us (see Phil. 1:6). We also have an opportunity to give thanks for God's purposes when our circumstances seem stagnant. When we face infertility, unwelcome singleness, or underemployment—when a hope deferred sickens the heart (see Prov. 13:12)—we give thanks that God is still working in a thousand ways that we cannot see.

What's more, we give thanks that God is working everywhere and at all times. If our current circumstances seem bleak, we have only to lift our eyes in order to find God's purposes being accomplished in the wider world. Among our friends and neighbors, God is bringing salvation. In the local church, God is proclaiming his gospel. On the mission field, God is establishing his church.

**Reflect:** Have you ever experienced an unwanted circumstance that later proved to be part of the Lord's good plan for you? How did you respond when you first encountered the circumstance? How did you feel when you realized God's kind purposes in it?

**Reflect:** Meditate on Psalm 33:11: "The counsel of the LORD stands forever, the plans of his heart to all generations." As you face life's uncertain and changing circumstances—or life's predictable and ordinary ones—give thanks for the eternal purposes of the Lord.

**Act:** Find out one way that God is accomplishing his purposes in the wider world: read a missionary update, ask someone in your church about a recent ministry project, email a friend in another state to find out how God is working where she is. Give thanks.

# DAY 23

# Giving Thanks for My Neighbor's Blessings

*Rejoice with those who rejoice, weep with those who weep. (Rom. 12:15)*

LIFE IS FILLED with opportunities to rejoice with others. Two friends invite you to their wedding. A coworker shares news of her pregnancy. Your neighbor starts his own business. A family member receives a community award. All around us, people are celebrating births and birthdays, promotions and retirements, graduations and new beginnings. And they want us to share in their joy.

But how can you smile at a wedding when you feel trapped in unwelcome singleness? How can you kiss that tiny baby's chubby cheeks when your own arms remain achingly empty year after year? How can you throw a party for a friend who just got accepted to the college where you were deferred? How can you extend your hand to the coworker who was promoted ahead of you? How can you send a congratulatory card to someone who got the life you always wanted?

1. *Give thanks for your neighbor's blessing because God commands it.* In today's verse, God commands us to "rejoice with those who rejoice." And, in the tenth commandment, God forbids us from coveting our neighbors' blessings (see Ex. 20:17). The Westminster Larger Catechism explains the duty of the tenth commandment this way: "[Having] such a charitable frame of the whole soul toward our neighbor . . . that all our inward motions . . . further all that good which is his."[1] We should love our neighbor so much that we want him to have as much good as possible.

2. *Give thanks because God is working in your neighbor's life (just as he is working in yours.)* Yesterday, we saw that God faithfully accomplishes his purposes in our lives and the lives of others. Our individual circumstances may appear radically different from the situation of our neighbor, but we trust that our neighbor's circumstances—just like our own—are carefully designed by God for his glory and our neighbor's good.

3. *Give thanks because, in the body of Christ, your neighbor's joy is your joy.* The work of Christ unites us to himself; it also unites us to everyone else who likewise belongs to Christ. In 1 Corinthians 12, we learn how this affects our experience of joy and blessing: "If one member suffers, all suffer together; if one member is honored, all rejoice together" (v. 26). Because the body is one, the joy of an individual member becomes the joy of every member. When God blesses a fellow member of his church, God blesses you.

**Reflect:** Think of a time when someone else rejoiced with you in your blessing, even when it was probably difficult. What made your friend's selfless joy particularly precious?

**Reflect:** Read John 17. Hours before his crucifixion, Jesus prays for his disciples and for all Christians. He asks the Father to grant them security (see vv. 11–12), though he himself would shortly be cut off from the Father. He asks the Father to give them unity (see vv. 20–23), though he himself would be betrayed and abandoned by his friends. He asks the Father to give them glory (see v. 22), though he himself would face complete humiliation. Be encouraged that this same Jesus is powerfully at work in you to enable you to rejoice in others' blessings.

**Act:** What kinds of celebrations are the hardest for you? Ask the Lord to remind you of the three reasons to give thanks the next time you have an opportunity to share in someone else's joy.

# PURSUING
# CONTENTMENT
# IN SPECIFIC
# CIRCUMSTANCES

# DAY 24

# Work and Responsibilities

*Whatever you do, work heartily, as for the Lord and not for men, knowing that from the Lord you will receive the inheritance as your reward. You are serving the Lord Christ. (Col. 3:23–24)*

DANIEL WAS A young man who was forcibly taken from his Israelite family and brought to the pagan courts of Nebuchadnezzar of Babylon. There he was trained in the language and literature of the Chaldeans for three years. After his education was complete, Daniel was assigned a place in the king's court as one of his advisors (see Dan. 1:3–5, 19–20). His job was demanding and dangerous, he worked every day for the enemy of his people, and he had no choice in the matter. And yet, Daniel says, "I rose and went about the king's business" (Dan. 8:27). On Monday morning, Daniel trusted God and went to work.

The first thing we should know about work is that it is a good gift given by God. In the newly created world, before sin had tainted anything, God gave Adam and Eve work to do: "The LORD God took the man and put him in the garden of Eden to work it and keep it" (Gen. 2:15). At the end of the sixth day, God surveyed his completed creation—including work—and pronounced it "very good" (Gen. 1:31). Any work that is not inherently sinful—whether paid or unpaid, skilled or unskilled, full-time or part-time or occasional—is good.

Sadly, after man's fall into sin, "thorns and thistles," "sweat," and "pain" also became part of all our work (Gen. 3:17–19). Because of Adam's sin, things break, crops fail, shipments disappear, and deadlines loom. If you find yourself doing a job you don't enjoy, and are attempting tasks with little success for an employer who is a sinner, you are experiencing the effects of a fallen world.

Work is good, work is fallen, and, in Christ, work is redeemed for God's glory and our good. Our verses today reorient the focus of our work. Paul instructs us to "work heartily, as for the Lord and not for men" (v. 23). Work is not ultimately about whether people respect us, whether our employer values us, or even whether we feel fulfilled in what we do. Work is about "serving the Lord Christ" (v. 24). As we do our best—with "sincerity of heart" (Col. 3:22)—in the situation where we have been placed, the Lord is glorified.

Work is also not ultimately about a monthly paycheck. "From the Lord," writes Paul, "you will receive the inheritance as your reward" (v. 24). The diligent worker who serves the Lord receives a heavenly reward. And all work ("whatever you do" v. 23)— whether cleaning toilets or managing stock portfolios—is an opportunity to please the Lord.

At the end of the workday, you may feel that your work has been meaningless or fruitless. But the Lord assures you that in his sight it is not.

**Reflect:** Thinking back over your work history, what are some opportunities you have had to bring glory to God even in undesirable jobs? How does God's faithfulness to you in the past give you encouragement for your current responsibilities?

**Reflect:** Read Luke 1:26–56. In this passage, Mary is given a job that she has not sought. It is a responsibility that will bring her both trouble and sorrow, and it is one for which she feels ill equipped. Ask the Lord to give you the grace to say with Mary, "I am the servant of the Lord; let it be to me according to your word" (v. 38).

**Act:** Memorize Colossians 3:23–24.

# DAY 25

# Money and Possessions

*As for the rich in this present age, charge them not to be haughty, nor to set their hopes on the uncertainty of riches, but on God, who richly provides us with everything to enjoy. They are to do good, to be rich in good works, to be generous and ready to share, thus storing up treasure for themselves as a good foundation for the future, so that they may take hold of that which is truly life. (1 Tim. 6:17–19)*

DARLENE DEIBLER ROSE served as a missionary to the Netherlands East Indies during World War II. A newlywed, Rose had selected a few treasured possessions to carry with her into the jungle; but, when the Japanese invaded, many of her belongings were stolen or destroyed. "My trunks of wedding gifts were dragged into the yard and the locks forced. Whatever the soldiers didn't want they scattered about the driveway. Our new refrigerator was carried outside by several Japanese who, one-two-three, threw it so hard that when it crashed on the gravel, the door flew open and irreparable damage was done to it. Bit by bit treasured keepsakes and souvenirs were being wrested from me."[1] As Rose watched her earthly possessions disappear, the Lord taught her a far more valuable lesson: "Whatever He allowed us of creature comforts, we were free to enjoy. If He chose to allow others to take them from us, that was His prerogative."[2]

As we have already seen, God is the one who provides us with all that we really need, and he is our greatest treasure. This framework enables us to pursue contentment with our money and possessions, whatever amount of them we may have.

Paul writes to Timothy in today's verses that all our possessions are provided by God for us to freely enjoy (see v. 17). If you have a favorite coffee mug or a comfortable chair or a trusty umbrella, those are God's good gifts to you. You may happily use those things while thanking God for his kindness.

Knowing that our possessions are gifts from God enables us to see ourselves as stewards rather than owners.[3] The dollars in our bank account and the items in our home are given by God, and God alone has ultimate authority over how they are used. We are simply entrusted with them for as long as he gives them to us, so that he might be glorified.

And this, in turn, allows us to "be generous and ready to share" (v. 18). We can happily share our possessions for the good of the kingdom and the work of the ministry, because we know that doing so will please God. Instead of anxiously grasping our piggy banks, we "take hold of that which is truly life" (v. 19).

**Reflect:** What is your favorite possession? Do you make a habit of enjoying it with thanksgiving to God?

**Reflect:** Read Acts 2:42–47. What did the first-century believers do with their money and possessions (see v. 45)? Do you think they shared gladly or grudgingly (see v. 46)? What effect did their radical generosity have on the people around them who witnessed it (see v. 47)?

**Act:** Today, as you check your bank account balance and use the items in your home, remind yourself that you are simply stewarding these things for God's glory. Ask God to teach you to hold your possessions loosely and to always be ready to exchange them for a better—eternal!—treasure.

# DAY 26

# Relationships and Family

*Put not your trust in princes, in a son of man, in whom there*
*is no salvation. . . . The LORD watches over the sojourners; he*
*upholds the widow and the fatherless. (Ps. 146:3, 9)*

IN 1873, HORATIO SPAFFORD sent his wife and four daughters on a transatlantic ship bound for Europe, intending to follow them a few days later. But, mid-voyage, their ship collided with another and sank in just twelve minutes. When the few survivors finally landed in Wales, Mrs. Spafford cabled her husband, "Saved alone." As a grieving Spafford traveled to meet his wife, his ship passed over the spot where his children had perished. There Spafford wrote the words to the now-famous hymn, "It Is Well with My Soul."[1]

Though the hymn begins with acknowledgement of grief ("when sorrows like sea billows roll,") each verse moves the singer toward ultimate peace and security in Christ's atoning work ("my sin . . . is nailed to the cross and I bear it no more") and the certainty of his second coming ("Lord, haste the day when the faith shall be sight.") Only when our hope is in those things can we sing with conviction, "It is well, it is well with my soul."[2]

In this fallen world, relational griefs are familiar. Some of us, like Spafford, have experienced the sudden death of family members. Others have faced unwelcome singleness, divorce, infertility, loneliness, betrayal, or estrangement. We may have wanted a storybook family and friends, but we feel disappointment instead.

Our desire for human relationships is good. When God set the first man in the good garden, he acknowledged that it was "not good" for Adam to be alone, and he created Eve as a companion for him (Gen. 2:18). Our desire for human relationships is good, but it is not ultimate. God brought Adam and Eve together so that they might together work and serve.[3] And the same God caused the apostle Paul to remain single so that he might single-mindedly work and serve (see 1 Cor. 7:7, 32–35). God has carefully designed the specific circumstances of our human relationships so that we may best serve him.

Today's verses remind us that human relationships often fail. Leaders let us down. Parents and spouses come to the end of their days. But we are not forsaken: "The LORD watches over the sojourners; he upholds the widow and the fatherless" (v. 9). The Lord who was himself abandoned by his friends at the moment of his death on the cross will never abandon us. Though we may be separated from friends and family, nothing—nothing!—can separate us from the love of God in Christ (see Rom. 8:38–39).

**Reflect:** In what ways have you "put . . . your trust in princes" (Ps. 146:3), expecting that your relationships with other people will provide ultimate security? How has this approach failed you in the past?

**Reflect:** Read Psalm 27. Note the various ways that David is experiencing relational pain and disappointment (see vv. 2, 3, 10, 12). In the midst of his sadness, where does David still find joy (see vv. 1, 8, 11, 13–14)? What is the "one thing" that is David's greatest desire and the source of his abiding contentment (see vv. 4–6)?

**Act:** Find the words to Spafford's hymn, "It Is Well with My Soul." Sing it, bringing your relational disappointments to the Lord and allowing the verses to draw your heart and mind toward your ultimate security in Christ.

# DAY 27

# Status and Recognition

*"But whoever would be great among you must be your servant,*
*and whoever would be first among you must be slave of all. For*
*even the Son of Man came not to be served but to serve, and to*
*give his life as a ransom for many." (Mark 10:43–45)*

C. H. SPURGEON was arguably the most well-known preacher of the nineteenth century. He routinely preached to crowds of over ten thousand, and his published sermons were widely distributed. Even today, his work continues to be read and appreciated. By contrast, his wife Susannah had little public presence; she spent her days attending to her famous husband's needs and to the needs of their children.

Susannah later wrote, "I do not take any credit to myself for this; it was the Lord's will concerning me, and He saw to it that I received the necessary training whereby, in after years, I could cheerfully surrender His chosen servant to the incessant demands of his ministry, his literary work, and the multiplied labours of his exceptionally busy life."[1]

Most of us will never be famous, will never receive a Nobel prize or a Pulitzer, will never be stalked by paparazzi or featured on the front page of the *New York Times*. We won't find our work highlighted in a museum retrospective or lauded in a biopic. We aren't usually described with words like "significant" and "vital." Honestly, most of us will barely receive a quick "thanks" from our employer or our kids today.

It can be tempting to become discontent when it feels like our work goes unnoticed. This was the situation in today's verses. James and John, two of Jesus's disciples, wanted Jesus to promise them public recognition in eternity. They believed that they had done good work and should have places of honor next to the throne in heaven. But Jesus's answer to their request turns their idea of status on its head: "Whoever would be great among you must be your servant" (v. 43). In this, we imitate our Lord Jesus, who "came not to be served but to serve" (v. 45).

This does not mean that we entirely give up the goal of recognition. It means that we look for our recognition from somewhere higher than the people around us. We give and pray and fast and serve in the sight of a loving Father who "sees in secret" and will richly reward us (Matt. 6:4, 6, 18).

**Reflect:** C. H. Spurgeon once wrote to Susannah, "None know how grateful I am to God for you. In all I have ever done for Him, you have a large share, for in making me so happy you have fitted me for service."[2] What is an example of a godly cause in which you have "a large share" because of your support? How does it encourage you that your prayers or giving or quiet words are vital to Christ's kingdom?

**Reflect:** Read Isaiah 52:13–53:12. Notice all the ways that Christ was brought low. Remember that you serve a Savior who gave up his right to earthly status and recognition so that you might be accounted righteous (see v. 11).

**Act:** Anna Waring's beloved hymn-prayer asks God to make her "content to fill a little space, if thou be glorified."[3] Today, find joy in occupying "a little space" where you can bring glory to the God who sees.

# DAY 28

# Gifts and Opportunities

*For the body does not consist of one member but of many. . . . But as it is, God arranged the members in the body, each one of them, as he chose. If all were a single member, where would the body be? As it is, there are many parts, yet one body. (1 Cor. 12:14, 18–20)*

CARL TRUEMAN EARNED A PhD from Aberdeen University and is a professor and prolific author. Trueman also spent years assisting his wife in a children's Sunday school class.[1] On Sunday mornings, this man who had delivered lectures at prestigious institutions could be found sitting on a tiny plastic chair, pouring cups of apple juice, and handing out crayons. In an article, Trueman explained this unlikely use of his gifts: "What role does the Ph.D. student or the professor play in the local church? Do they consider their role restricted, for example, to teaching the adult Sunday school or leading a Bible study, such that . . . the clean-up team or the tea rota or the nursery are considered off-limits and infra dig? On the contrary, the church is the church, and it is a privilege for anyone to be involved at any level in any of her manifold activities."[2]

When we consider our gifts and the opportunities we have to exercise those gifts, we can be tempted to two different types of discontent. Sometimes we recognize our own gifts and chafe against the limited opportunities we have to use them. The mother of young children, the widow in a nursing home, the underemployed worker, the church member assigned to nursery duty—all can feel frustrated that their gifts seem to languish unused.

At other times, we compare our gifts to those that the Lord has given to others, and we grumble that we are not able to do what others can. We (wrongly) believe that if only we were gifted like the person in the next pew, we would be satisfied.

Today's verses reorient our understanding of our gifts (and the opportunities we have to use them) by placing our gifts in the context of Christ's body, the church. In 1 Corinthians 12, Paul reminds us that the ultimate source of our gifts is God himself. The "same God" gives gifts and service and "empowers them all in everyone" (see vv. 4–6). God gives "varieties of gifts" (v. 4) for "the common good" (v. 7).

We count it no small thing to serve the church in whatever way we can be of use. In fact, before we were even born, God prepared specific opportunities for us to serve his body (see Eph. 2:10).

You are not unnoticed or unused by God. Whatever your gifts, you have been placed in your local church exactly according to God's will (see 1 Cor. 12:18). And you have been placed there for a glorious goal: the praise of Christ in the building up of the body.

**Reflect:** What gifts has the Lord given you? Thank him for those gifts. What opportunities has he given you to serve his body? Thank him for those opportunities.

**Reflect:** Read Luke 10:17–20. The disciples were given the spectacular ability to cast out demons, but Jesus tells them that, more than celebrating this gift, they should rejoice in their salvation. Thank God today that "your [name is] written in heaven" (v. 20).

**Act:** Consider the needs of your local church. What ministries does your church struggle to find volunteers for? Are you willing to serve Christ and his body in this way?

# DAY 29

# Health and Abilities

*But [God] said to me, "My grace is sufficient for you, for my power is
made perfect in weakness." Therefore I will boast all the more gladly of my
weaknesses, so that the power of Christ may rest upon me. (2 Cor. 12:9)*

IN 1967, SEVENTEEN-YEAR-OLD Joni Eareckson suffered
a diving accident that left her a quadriplegic—bound to a wheelchair and unable to complete tasks with her arms and hands. Fifty
years later, she said in an interview, "There really are more important things in life than walking. There are more important things
in life than having the use of your hands. And that is having a heart
that's free of the grip of sin and pride and self-centeredness."[1]

Joni's words may sound incredible to a society that idolizes
physical ability. In the logic of this world, athletes are our greatest heroes and the terminally ill are our greatest embarrassment.
To many Christians, too, finding contentment in the midst of
cancer, clinical depression, or even a two-week-long cold seems
extraordinary.

And yet today's verse, which describes the experience of the
apostle Paul as he suffered a "thorn . . . in the flesh" (2 Cor. 12:7),
provides hope for us when we are sick, tired, and weak. Like Paul,
we can rest on God's promise to be at work in us through our
limitations.

Our physical illness is never simply a matter of germs and
genetics. Passages like 2 Corinthians 1:3–7 show us that our suffering is the careful tool of a loving God, designed for our good.
By it, we know ourselves to be weak and dependent on his abundant mercies. By it, we gain understanding of the sufferings of
Christ on our behalf. By it, we have an opportunity to receive
comfort from God. By it, we are equipped to comfort others who

also suffer. And by it, we bring glory to God as we patiently submit to the work he is doing in us.

This does not mean that we stop praying for healing. In fact, James 5:13–16 commands us to bring our physical illnesses to the Lord. But it does mean that we pray with an attitude of submission—the same submission that Christ demonstrated when he prayed, "Not as I will, but as you will" (Matt. 26:39)—resting in the knowledge that God does all things well.

We can expect Christ to make us content and to enable us to declare boldly with Paul, "For the sake of Christ, then, I am content with weaknesses, insults, hardships, persecutions, and calamities. For when I am weak, then I am strong" (2 Cor. 12:10).

**Reflect:** What physical afflictions do you suffer? What is their impact on your ability to do the things you would like to do? How could these afflictions be a tool used by God for his glory and your good? Read 2 Corinthians 1:3–7. Make a list of all the ways that Paul finds God's good purpose in his sufferings.

**Reflect:** When you pray for healing, remember that you are bringing your request to the Savior who suffered and died for the good of your eternal soul.

**Act:** As you encounter the limitations of your physical body, prayerfully lament the painful effects of sin in this fallen world, praise Christ for his willingness to suffer for your sake, and ask the Lord to teach you the lesson he taught Paul: "My grace is sufficient for you, for my power is made perfect in weakness." (2 Cor. 12:9).

# DAY 30

# Beauty and Appearance

*But let your adorning be the hidden person of the heart*
*with the imperishable beauty of a gentle and quiet spirit,*
*which in God's sight is very precious. (1 Peter 3:4)*

WHEN AMY CARMICHAEL was three years old, she earnestly
prayed that the Lord would change her brown eyes to blue. She
went to bed, confidently expecting that she would awaken to see
blue eyes staring out of the mirror at her. The Lord did not grant
her request, and Carmichael's eyes remained brown.[1]

Many years later, serving as a missionary in India, Carmichael
had an opportunity to meet secretly with a notorious criminal
who had become a Christian. She hoped to persuade him to own
Christ publicly and give himself up. Dressing carefully for the dangerous nighttime rendezvous, Carmichael "stained her face and
hands, put on her darkest sari," and was "thankful for the brown
eyes she had once besought God to exchange for blue ones."[2]

Like Amy Carmichael, most of us can think of something (or
several somethings) that we would like to change about our appearance. We want to be taller or shorter, to lose weight or to gain it,
to have a smaller nose or bigger eyes or less conspicuous ears.
We look in the mirror and grumble about another bad hair day.
We look in the closet and grumble that we have nothing to wear.

In a world where appearance is extremely important—even
ultimate—it can be easy to fall into discontent with our own. Our
teeth will never be as white nor our legs as toned as the images
we see in every commercial and storefront and television show.
And when our friends and coworkers dedicate countless dollars
and hours to the pursuit of greater beauty, we might believe that
we should too.

When Samuel stood in Jesse's home to anoint a new king, he assumed that the good-looking Eliab must be the chosen one. Yet the Lord redirected Samuel's priorities: "For the LORD sees not as man sees: man looks on the outward appearance, but the LORD looks on the heart" (1 Sam. 16:7).

Though the Bible does not dismiss physical beauty, today's verse reminds us that God places a far higher priority on our hearts. It is "the hidden person of the heart" that most defines who we are in the eyes of the Lord. Our physical appearance, like every other circumstance of our lives, is intended for the service of God.

As Jerry Bridges writes about Psalm 139, "God so directed the DNA and other biological factors that determine our physical makeup that the psalmist can say, 'God formed me in my mother's womb.' That is an incredible thought! You and I are who we are physically because that is the way God made us. And He made us the way we are because that is how we can best fulfill His plan for our lives."[3]

**Reflect:** What messages in the wider culture or in your community contribute to your discontent with your appearance? What messages in the Bible reorient your emphasis on beauty (see 1 Sam. 16:7; Ps. 139; 1 Peter 3:4)?

**Reflect:** Think of people you know who are diligently serving God. As they come to mind, notice how their physical appearance seems unimportant compared to their godly character.

**Act:** As you look in the mirror today, thank the Lord for creating you. Thank him for designing every detail of your appearance for his purposes. Ask him to help you use your physical body to serve him.

# DAY 31

# I Have Learned to Be Content

*Not that I am speaking of being in need, for I have learned in whatever
situation I am to be content. I know how to be brought low, and I
know how to abound. In any and every circumstance, I have learned
the secret of facing plenty and hunger, abundance and need. I can
do all things through him who strengthens me. (Phil. 4:11–13)*

THE APOSTLE PAUL did not enjoy a life of easy circumstances.

> Five times I received at the hands of the Jews the forty lashes
> less one. Three times I was beaten with rods. Once I was stoned.
> Three times I was shipwrecked; a night and a day I was adrift
> at sea; on frequent journeys, in danger from rivers, danger
> from robbers, danger from my own people, danger from Gen-
> tiles, danger in the city, danger in the wilderness, danger at sea,
> danger from false brothers; in toil and hardship, through many
> a sleepless night, in hunger and thirst, often without food, in
> cold and exposure. And, apart from other things, there is the
> daily pressure on me of my anxiety for all the churches. (2 Cor.
> 11:24–28)

Wherever he went, he faced difficulty. He was mistreated by his
enemies and intentionally misunderstood by those who should
have been his friends (see 2 Peter 3:16). He regularly encountered "afflictions, hardships, calamities, beatings, imprisonments,
riots, labors, sleepless nights, [and] hunger" (2 Cor. 6:4–5). He
was often alone and rarely comfortable, and his life was almost
always at risk.

And yet, in today's verses, Paul says sincerely, "I have learned
in whatever situation I am to be content" (Phil. 4:11). Paul
knew the truth we have learned this month: contentment is

not dependent on the changing circumstances of life but on the unchanging goodness of our Lord.

This truth equips us to correctly understand our present situation. Paul could accept imprisonment, and we can accept today's health diagnosis or bank statement or to-do list, because we trust that it is given by a sovereign God for our good and his glory.

This truth also equips us to face every unknown situation that awaits us in the future. Paul writes that he "can do all things through him who strengthens me" (Phil. 4:13); his contentment for today—and for tomorrow—rests on a God who is "the same yesterday and today and forever" (Heb. 13:8). We do not know what the coming days will hold—what disappointments, frustrations, and losses—but the loving care of our all-powerful God is certain.

In our pursuit of contentment, we look for help from Christ himself (see Phil. 4:13), the only perfectly content man. He is the one who was rich and yet became poor, denying himself every comfortable circumstance, so that we could share the lasting riches of his glorious inheritance in eternity (see 2 Cor. 8:9).

**Reflect:** What have you learned about contentment this month? What things did you already know but needed to be reminded of? What things were new concepts to you?

**Reflect:** Speaking of Christ, John the Baptist said, "He must increase, but I must decrease" (John 3:30). When we focus less on ourselves and our circumstances and more on our Christ and his glory, we will find contentment. Make it your life's aim to magnify Christ alone.

**Act:** Memorize Philippians 4:13: "I can do all things through him who strengthens me." As you pursue contentment in the coming days, remember that you have very great help from your very great Savior.

# Conclusion

TOMORROW BEGINS A NEW DAY. The sun will come up, the alarm will sound, the calendar will advance, and your life will go on. For some of us, this new day will bring a fresh set of events—new responsibilities, new relationships, new trials, new expectations. For others, this day will be much like the day before and the day before that and the day before that. But whether the Lord brings us unexpected circumstances or asks us to remain faithful in familiar ones, we trust that he will bring only what is best.

With each new day and month and year, God will be at work. He will accomplish his grand purposes of exalting Christ, bringing sinners to salvation, and making his children more like his Son—and he will do it in all the moments of all your days.

Tomorrow, as you rise to a new day, make the words of this Puritan prayer your own:

> Let me learn by paradox
>> that the way down is the way up,
>> that to be low is to be high,
>> that the broken heart is the healed heart,
>> that the contrite spirit is the rejoicing spirit,
>> that the repenting soul is the victorious soul,
>> that to have nothing is to possess all,
>> that to bear the cross is to wear the crown,
>> that to give is to receive,
>> that the valley is the place of vision.[1]

# Notes

### Tips for Reading This Devotional
1. Jonathan Leeman, *Reverberation: How God's Word Brings Light, Freedom, and Action to His People* (Chicago: Moody, 2011), 19.

### Day 1: Abundant Life
1. Jeremiah Burroughs, *The Rare Jewel of Christian Contentment* (1648; repr., Carlisle, PA: Banner of Truth Trust, 2000), 19.

### Day 2: A Weightless Heart
1. John Bunyan, *The Pilgrim's Progress: From This World to That Which Is to Come Delivered Under the Similitude of a Dream Wherein Is Discovered the Manner of His Setting Out, His Dangerous Journey, and Safe Arrival at the Desired Country* (1678; repr., New York: Houghton Mifflin, 1896), 39–40.
2. Christopher Ash, *Discovering the Joy of a Clear Conscience* (London: Inter-Varsity Press, 2012; repr., Phillipsburg, NJ: P&R Publishing, 2014), 176–77.

### Day 3: Contentment Is Great Gain
1. Jeremiah Burroughs, *The Rare Jewel of Christian Contentment* (1648; repr., Carlisle, PA: Banner of Truth Trust, 2000), 118–35.

### Day 4: Christ, Our Encouragement
1. See *Human Planet*, season 1, episode 1, "Oceans—Into the Blue," aired January 13, 2011, on BBC, https://www.bbc.co.uk/programmes/b00rrd81.
2. Heidelberg Catechism, question and answer 1, available online from the Reformed Church in America, https://www.rca.org/resources/heidelbergcatechism.

### Day 8: I Have Nothing
1. John Calvin, *Institutes of the Christian Religion*, ed. John T. McNeill, trans. Ford Lewis Battles (Philadelphia: Westminster Press, 1960), 1.1.1.

**Day 11: God's Care for Me Is More Certain Than Life's Changing Circumstances**

1. *New World Encyclopedia*, s.v. "John D. Rockefeller," last modified August 25, 2016, 18:10, http://www.newworldencyclopedia.org /p/index.php?title=John_D._Rockefeller&oldid=998940.
2. John Newton, "Glorious Things of Thee Are Spoken," 1779.

**Day 12: The Circumstances of My Life Are Carefully Designed for the Good of My Undying Soul**

1. "These troubles, that lie heavy, never come upon us but when we have need, and never stay any longer than needs must" (Matthew Henry, *Matthew Henry's Commentary*, vol. 6, *Acts to Revelation* [1710; repr., Peabody, MA: Hendrikson, 1991], 811).

**Day 13: Desire Must Be Trained**

1. Melissa B. Kruger, *The Envy of Eve: Finding Contentment in a Covetous World* (Tain, UK: Christian Focus Publications, 2012), 21.
2. Westminster Larger Catechism, answer 148.

**Day 14: God Sets the Priorities for My Desires**

1. See Louis Menand, "What It Is Like to Like: Art and Taste in the Age of the Internet," *The New Yorker*, June 20, 2016, 73–76.
2. Menand, 74.

**Day 15: Desiring God's Glory**

1. Westminster Shorter Catechism, answer 98.
2. Jeremiah Burroughs, *The Rare Jewel of Christian Contentment* (1648; repr., Carlisle, PA: Banner of Truth Trust, 2000), 54.

**Day 16: Desiring Daily Provision from God's Hand**

1. *First Catechism: Teaching Children Bible Truths* (2003; repr., Suwanee, GA: Great Commission Publications, 2012), question 121.

**Day 17: Desiring Holiness**

1. Quoted in Carl R. Trueman, *Luther on the Christian Life: Cross and Freedom* (Wheaton, IL: Crossway, 2015), 45–46.
2. William B. Barcley, *The Secret of Contentment* (Phillipsburg, NJ: P&R Publishing), 100.
3. Andrew Bonar, *The Life and Remains, Letters, Lectures, and Poems*

*of the Rev. Robert Murray McCheyne* (New York: Robert Carter & Brothers, 1866), 142.

### Day 18: Righteous Discontent

1. George L. Prentiss, *The Life of Elizabeth Prentiss, Author of Stepping Heavenward*, rev. ed. (New York: Randolph, 1898), 2:178.
2. William B. Barcley, *The Secret of Contentment* (Phillipsburg, NJ: P&R Publishing), 68.
3. Jeremiah Burroughs, *The Rare Jewel of Christian Contentment* (1648; repr., Carlisle, PA: Banner of Truth Trust, 2000), 42.

### Day 19: Thanksgiving Is God's Will for Me

1. David W. Pao, *Thanksgiving: An Investigation of a Pauline Theme* (Downers Grove, IL: InterVarsity Press, 2002), 57.

### Day 20: Giving Thanks for Salvation

1. J. Todd Billings, *Union with Christ: Reframing Theology and Ministry for the Church* (Grand Rapids: Baker Academic, 2011), 25; emphasis in original.

### Day 21: Giving Thanks for Daily Provision

1. "The Story of 'Grace': A Much-Loved World Famous Picture," Grace by Enstrom, accessed June 4, 2018, http://www.graceby enstrom.com/history.html.
2. *First Catechism: Teaching Children Bible Truths* (2003; repr., Suwanee, GA: Great Commission Publications, 2012), answer 121.

### Day 22: Giving Thanks for God's Purposes

1. See Corrie Ten Boom, "Ravensbruck," chap. 13 in *The Hiding Place* (Ulrichsville, OH: Barbour Publishing, 1971).

### Day 23: Giving Thanks for My Neighbor's Blessings

1. Westminster Larger Catechism, answer 147.

### Day 25: Money and Possessions

1. Darlene Deibler Rose, *Evidence Not Seen: A Woman's Miraculous Faith in the Jungles of World War II* (New York: Harper One, 1988), 48.
2. Rose, 48.
3. See Melissa B. Kruger, *The Envy of Eve: Finding Contentment in a Covetous World* (Tain, UK: Christian Focus Publications, 2012), 136.

**Day 26: Relationships and Family**
1. See Kenneth W. Osbeck, *101 Hymn Stories: The Inspiring True Stories Behind 101 Favorite Hymns* (Grand Rapids: Kregel, 1982), 127.
2. Horatio G. Spafford, "It Is Well with My Soul," 1873.
3. See Christopher Ash, *Marriage: Sex in the Service of God* (Vancouver, BC: Regent College Publishing, 2003), 119–22.

**Day 27: Status and Recognition**
1. Susannah Spurgeon, *C.H. Spurgeon's Autobiography: Compiled from His Diary, Letters, and Records by His Wife and His Private Secretary*, vol. 2, *1854–1860* (London: Passmore and Alabaster, 1899), 16.
2. Spurgeon, 17.
3. Anna L. Waring, "Father, I Know That All My Life," 1850.

**Day 28: Gifts and Opportunities**
1. See Carl R. Trueman, *Luther on the Christian Life: Cross and Freedom* (Wheaton, IL: Crossway, 2015), 111.
2. Carl Trueman, "The Way of the Christian Academic," *Themelios* 33, no. 3 (December 2008): 5.

**Day 29: Health and Abilities**
1. Kelli B. Trujillo, "After 50 Years in a Wheelchair, I Still Walk with Jesus," *Christianity Today*, July 28, 2017, http://www.christianity today.com/women/2017/july/joni-eareckson-tada-fifty-years-wheelchair-walk-jesus.html.

**Day 30: Beauty and Appearance**
1. See Elisabeth Elliot, *A Chance to Die: The Life and Legacy of Amy Carmichael* (Old Tappan, NJ: Fleming H. Revell, 1987), 24–25.
2. Elliot, 260.
3. Jerry Bridges, *Respectable Sins: Confronting the Sins We Tolerate* (Colorado Springs: NavPress, 2010), 95–96.

**Conclusion**
1. Arthur Bennett, ed., *The Valley of Vision: A Collection of Puritan Prayers and Devotions* (1975; repr., Carlisle, PA: The Banner of Truth Trust, 2002), xxiv.

# Suggested Resources for the Fight

Barcley, William B. *The Secret of Contentment*. Phillipsburg, NJ: P&R Publishing, 2010. [This book distills the wisdom of two older writers (Jeremiah Burroughs and Thomas Watson) on contentment, combining and expanding their biblical counsel for the good of readers. Each chapter also includes useful questions for discussion.]

Burroughs, Jeremiah. *The Rare Jewel of Christian Contentment*. 1648. Reprint, Carlisle, PA: Banner of Truth Trust, 2000. [Puritan Jeremiah Burroughs's treatment of contentment is practical, gracious, and thoroughly biblical. Don't let the 1648 publication date put you off—Burroughs's wisdom for cultivating contentment is just as relevant and helpful today as it was 350 years ago.]

Kruger, Melissa B. *The Envy of Eve: Finding Contentment in a Covetous World*. Tain, UK: Christian Focus Publications, 2012. [Melissa Kruger tackles one of discontent's nasty companions: covetousness. Using the examples of five different biblical characters, she uncovers the sin of envy and details its remedy in Christ.]

The Westminster Larger Catechism. In *The Westminster Confession of Faith Together with the Larger Catechism and the Shorter Catechism with Scripture Proofs*. 3rd ed. Lawrenceville, GA: Committee for Christian Education and Publications, 1990. See Q&A 144–146. [For unmasking sin and driving us to Christ, the Larger Catechism's explanation of the ten commandments is indispensable. In questions 144–146, the Catechism reveals what God is both commanding and forbidding when he says "you shall not covet" (Ex. 20:17).]

## BIBLICAL COUNSELING COALITION

The Biblical Counseling Coalition (BCC) is passionate about enhancing and advancing biblical counseling globally. We accomplish this through broadcasting, connecting, and collaborating.

**Broadcasting** promotes gospel-centered biblical counseling ministries and resources to bring hope and healing to hurting people around the world. We promote biblical counseling in a number of ways: through our *15:14* podcast, website (biblicalcounselingcoalition.org), partner ministry, conference attendance, and personal relationships.

**Connecting** biblical counselors and biblical counseling ministries is a central component of the BCC. The BCC was founded by leaders in the biblical counseling movement who saw the need for and the power behind building a strong global network of biblical counselors. We introduce individuals and ministries to one another to establish gospel-centered relationships.

**Collaboration** is the natural outgrowth of our connecting efforts. We truly believe that biblical counselors and ministries can accomplish more by working together. The BCC Confessional Statement, which is a clear and comprehensive definition of biblical counseling, was created through the cooperative effort of over thirty leading biblical counselors. The BCC has also published a three-part series of multi-contributor works that bring theological wisdom and practical expertise to pastors, church leaders, counseling practitioners, and students. Each year we are able to facilitate the production of numerous resources, including books, articles, videos, audio resources, and a host of other helps for biblical counselors. Working together allows us to provide robust resources and develop best practices in biblical counseling so that we can hone the ministry of soul care in the church.

To learn more about the BCC, visit biblicalcounselingcoalition.org.